Saint Joseph

Saint Joseph

The Father of Jesus
in a Fatherless Society

LEONARDO BOFF

TRANSLATED BY
Alexandre Guilherme

CASCADE *Books* • Eugene, Oregon

SAINT JOSEPH
The Father of Jesus in a Fatherless Society

Copyright © 2009 Leonardo Boff. Translation copyright © 2009 Alexandre
Guilherme. All rights reserved. Except for brief quotations in critical publications
or reviews, no part of this book may be reproduced in any manner without
prior written permission from the publisher. Write: Permissions, Wipf and Stock
Publishers, 199 W. 8th Ave., Eugene, OR 97401.

Cascade Books
A Division of Wipf and Stock Publishers
199 W. 8th Ave., Suite 3
Eugene, OR 97401

www.wipfandstock.com

ISBN 13: 978-1-49821-123-9

Cataloging-in-Publication data:

Boff, Leonardo.
    Saint Joseph : the father of Jesus in a fatherless society / Leonardo Boff. Translated
by Alexandre Guilherme.

    viii + 180 p. ; 23 cm.

    Includes bibliographical references and index.

    Translated from the Portugese.

    ISBN 13: 978-1-60608-007-8

    1. Joseph, Saint. 2. Hypostatic union. I. Guilherme, Alexandre. II. Coelho, Paulo.
III. Title.

BT690 B6413 2009

Manufactured in the U.S.A.

Contents

Foreword

Four out of the five times that the word *dream* appears in the New Testament are connected with Joseph. He is always being convinced by an angel to do exactly the opposite of what he was planning to do.

Do not abandon your wife. He certainly could have said something like: "What will the neighbors think?"

Go to Egypt. And again, St. Joseph could have thought something of the kind: "Do I have to do it just now, just as I have stabilized my life and that I have a family to support?"

But contrary to commonsense Joseph follows his dreams. He knows he has a destiny to fulfill: to protect and to support his family. Just as millions of anonymous Josephs, he seeks to handle the task at hand, even to the extent of following dreams that are sometimes beyond his comprehension. Later, his wife and one of his sons become the great references of Christianity. The third pillar of the family, however, the laborer, is only remembered in nativity scenes at the end of the year or by those who have a special devotion to him, as it is my case and as it is the case with Leonardo Boff.

Hence, a book about Joseph is a blessing because it reveals the laborer, the father, the person who follows dreams, the person who provides the bread so that his son can consecrate it. It shows the revolutionary who accepts being guided through an invisible world. It shows the protector and the wise man because without the family values inculcated by him all history could have been different.

I often read such aberrations as: "Jesus went to India to learn with the sages of the Himalayas." For me, every person learns from the task that is given by life, and Jesus learned while doing tables, chairs, and beds.

In the paths of ordinary people, in our pathway, are all the lessons that God wishes to give us every day, and it is enough to include the word *love* in the daily struggle to transform this struggle into a sacred task.

In my imagination I like to think of the table where Christ consecrated the bread and wine as being made by Joseph. Because there, in the table, was the hand of an anonymous carpenter, who earned his life with the sweat of his face and who, exactly because of this, allowed miracles to happen.

Paulo Coelho[1]

---

1. Translator's note: Paulo Coelho is a Brazilian novelist and the author of bestselling novels such as *The Alchemist, Brida, Zahir,* and *The Witch of Portobello.* His books have been sold in over 150 countries worldwide and he has received a number of literary awards such as the La Legion d'Honneur from France and the Grinzane Carvour from Italy.

The Gospel of Joseph

Saint Joseph did not leave us a single word. He delivered to us his silence and his example of a just man, of a hard worker, of a husband, of a father and of an educator. Let me list the passages in the New Testament that are concerned with him.

THE GENEALOGY OF HIS SON JESUS

In the long list of the forefathers of Jesus, Joseph is the last link. Matthew starts with Abraham and ends like this: "and Jacob the father of Joseph the husband of Mary, of whom Jesus was born, who is called the Christ." (Matt 1:16)

Luke starts with Joseph, whose father is not Jacob but Heli, and ends in Adam and in God. Luke says: "Jesus, when he began his ministry, was about thirty years of age, being the son (as was supposed) of Joseph . . ." (Luke 2:23)

THE ANNUNCIATION OF THE BIRTH OF HIS SON JESUS

Luke narrates the annunciation like this:

"In the sixth month the angel Gabriel was sent from God to a city of Galilee named Nazareth to a virgin betrothed to a man whose name was Joseph, of the house of David . . . and Mary said to the angel, 'How can this be, since I have no husband?'" (Luke 1:26–27, 34)

Matthew writes about it like this:

"When his mother Mary had been betrothed to Joseph, before they came together she was found to be with child of the Holy Spirit; and her husband Joseph, being a just man and unwilling to put her to shame, resolved to divorce her quietly. But as he considered this, behold, an angel of the Lord appeared to him in a dream, saying, 'Joseph, son of David, do not fear to take Mary for your wife, for that which is conceived in her is of the Holy Spirit; she will bear a son, and you shall call his name Jesus, for he will save his people from their sins' . . . when Joseph woke from sleep, he did as the angel of the Lord commanded him; he took his wife, but he knew her not until she had born a son; and he called his name Jesus." (Matt 1:18–21, 24–25)

THE BIRTH OF HIS SON JESUS

Luke narrates the birth of Jesus in the following manner:

"In those days a decree went out from Caesar Augustus that all the world should be enrolled. This was the first enrolment, when Quirinius was governor of Syria. And all went to be enrolled, each to his own city. And Joseph also went up from Galilee, from the city of Nazareth, to Judea, to the city of David, which was called Bethlehem, because he was of the house and lineage of David, to be enrolled with Mary, his betrothed, who was with child . . . the shepherds said to one another, 'Let us go over to Bethlehem and see this thing that has happened, which the Lord has made known to us.' And they went with haste, and found Mary and Joseph, and the babe lying in a manger." (Luke 2:1–5, 15–16)

THE FLIGHT TO EGYPT

"Now that they (Magi) had departed, behold, an angel of the Lord, appeared to Joseph in a dream and said, 'Rise, take the child and his mother to Egypt, and remain there till I tell you; for Herod is about to search for the child, to destroy him.' And he rose and took the child and his mother by night, and departed to Egypt, and remained there until the death of Herod." (Matt 2:13–15)

THE FAMILY MOVES TO NAZARETH

"But when Herod died, behold, an angel of the Lord appeared in a dream to Joseph in Egypt, saying, 'Rise, take the child and his mother, and go to the land of Israel, for those who sought the child's life are dead.' And he rose and took the child and his mother, and went to the land of Israel. But when he heard that Archelaus reigned over Judea in place of his father Herod, he was afraid to go there, and being warned in a dream he withdrew to the district of Galilee. And he went and dwelt in a city called Nazareth, that what was spoken by the prophets might be fulfilled, 'He shall be called a Nazarene.'" (Matt 2:19–23)

JESUS IS PRESENTED IN THE TEMPLE

"And when the time came for their purification according to the law of Moses, they brought him (Jesus) up to Jerusalem to present him to the Lord . . . the parents brought in the child Jesus, to do for him according to the custom of the law . . . And his father and mother marveled at what was said about him . . . And when they had performed everything according to the law of the Lord, they returned into Galilee, to their own city of Nazareth . . ." (Luke 2:22, 27, 33, 39)

JESUS AT THE AGE OF TWELVE IN THE TEMPLE

"Now his parents went to Jerusalem every year at the feast of the Passover. And when he (Jesus) was twelve years old, they went up according to custom; and when the feast was ended, as they were returning, the boy Jesus stayed behind in Jerusalem. His parents did not know it, but supposing him to be in the company they went a day's journey, and they sought him among their kinsfolk and acquaintances; and when they did not find him, they returned to Jerusalem seeking him. After three days they found him in the temple, sitting among the teachers, listening to them and asking them questions; and all who heard him were amazed at his understanding and his answers. And when they saw him they were astonished; and his mother said to him, 'Son, why have you treated us so? Behold, your father and I have been looking for you anxiously.' And he said to them, 'How is it that you sought me? Did you not know that I must be in my

Father's house?' . . . And he went down with them and came to Nazareth, and was obedient to them." (Matt 2:41–49, 51)

SON OF JOSEPH, THE CARPENTER

". . . and coming to his (Jesus) own country he taught them in their synagogue, so that they were astonished, and said, '. . . Is he not the carpenter's son? Is not his mother called Mary? And are not his brothers James and Joseph and Simon and Judas? And are not all his sisters with us?" (Matt 13:54–56)

"And all spoke well of him, and wondered at the gracious words which proceeded out of his mouth; and they said, 'Is not this Joseph's son?'" (Luke 4:22)

"Philip found Nathanael, and said to him, 'We have found him of whom Moses in the law and also the prophets wrote, Jesus of Nazareth, son of Joseph.' . . . The Jews then murmured at him, because he said, 'I am the bread which came down from heaven.' They said, 'Is not this Jesus, the son of Joseph, whose father and mother we know? How does he now say, 'I have come down from heaven?'" (John 1:45; 6:41–42)

1

How Does One Speak of Saint Joseph Today?

What can be said accurately about Saint Joseph? We do not have one single word from him. Our culture and theology are built to a great extent from spoken and written words. When these are not present memory fades away and intelligence is clouded, and we are then left with the imagination, which notoriously has neither censorship nor limits.

For this reason Saint Joseph has not yet found his place within theological reflections. He is like a piece of land that has strayed away from the theological continent, or even, it is as if he simply did not exist. He belongs more to the piety of the people than to the meditation of popes, of theologians, and of the educated strata of Christianity. Despite this, millions of people, institutions, and places take his name: Joseph.

RECOVERING THE FIGURE OF SAINT JOSEPH

In the past decades, however, there has been vigorous research concerning him, which is only comparable to what happened during the seventeenth century when throughout Christendom there emerged a significant meditative study of Saint Joseph. Practically all theologians turn him into an aspect of Christology or Mariology. When faced by Jesus and Mary he takes a secondary and complementary role. His mission is to provide security to the mother and to take care of the baby Jesus. When this function is fulfilled he could disappear from the picture, as in fact was done.

Sometimes theologians deal with Saint Joseph in an inarticulate and non-systematic way by placing him along with other subjects of revelation and theology. The figure of Saint Joseph is used to approach subjects such as the importance of the family, generally speaking, and of fatherhood. However, a devotional and pious approach prevails, which does not engage in a fecund dialogue with contributions made by the sciences within this important subject.

But I do not want to be one-sided here. There are a number of notable researchers and theologians, such as T. Stramatare in Italy, B. Llamera in Spain, R. Gauthier and P. Robert in Canada, F. Filas and L. Bourassa Perrota in the USA, H. Rondet and A. Doze in France, J. Stöhr and F. Brändle in Germany, among others. We have also seen the creation of some centers of research and archives of notable standing with their respective journals which are dedicated to the study of Saint Joseph (Josephology) and which have collated all available data that has been written on this subject down through the centuries. About twenty thousand titles of all types on this subject have been catalogued. There you can find very rich material, which is by and large of historical character, to improve the understanding and the systematization of thought about the father of Jesus and the husband of Mary.

I will make use of these whenever possible. I wish to thank here the Centre de Recherché et de Documentation of the Oratoire Saint-Joseph in Montreal, Canada, and especially its director, Pierre Robert, and his secretary, Katrine, for allowing me the use of its immense library, one of the best in this subject, so that I could do bibliographical research and have access to rare tomes and journals on Josephology. Without their kindness this book could not have been written given the peripheral conditions in which I live, far from metropolitan centers of research and publication.

THE OBJECTIVE OF MY REFLECTIONS

What is the task I propose to undertake? I propose to answer the question: Has Joseph a unique and singular relationship with the celestial Father to the extent that it could be said that he represents the personification of the Father? And once this question has been answered, then try to establish: What is his relation with the embodied Son, Jesus, and with Mary, his wife, over whom the Holy Spirit put his shadow? What is the meaning of the family Jesus–Mary–Joseph in relation to the divine Family Father–Son–Holy Spirit?

The fact that Joseph has not left us a single word, of receiving messages only through dreams, of being the silent figure of the New Testament, is neither an accident nor is it meaningless. This silence is loaded with a message, the meaning of which must be decoded. Saint Joseph is an artisan and not a rabbi. His hands are more meaningful than his mouth, his work more meaningful than his words.

The task of theology is to question about God and about all things in the light of God and this should not be done only from the perspective of biblical texts, of hereditary traditions and of doctrines that have been fixed by the ecclesiastical Magisterium, since these do not fully encapsulate God nor do they fully encompass revelation. The living God continues to communicate himself in history and for this reason is always larger, breaking through the barriers set by religions, by sacred texts, by doctrinal and theological authorities and by the mindset of people. For this reason it is important to search for God in creation as we understand it today as an immense process of ascending evolution, to search for God in human history, to search for God in the production of creative thinking itself.

God is a mysterious fountainhead and as such all knowledge and all words are insufficient. We are always challenged to take up the effort of trying to comprehend and understand God further, even when we are conscious that God will always continue to be a mystery.

Thus, what is important is to go beyond the limits that have been set by everything that has been so far said and traditionally established with regards to Saint Joseph—these are the outcome of piety, art, literature and meditation. It is always appropriate to place Saint Joseph and the human condition side by side and to try to discover the religious meaning that arises from this; and concretely speaking, it is crucial to bring Saint Joseph out of the marginal position in which he has been left and to provide him with the central role that he deserves.

It is necessary, however, to respect Saint Joseph's humility, which has been often violated by a Josephology of exaltation and of enumeration of privileges and virtues. This was the kind of discourse that prevailed among theologians, especially in the seventeenth century when the first treatises on Saint Joseph were written. This flattering way of speaking about Saint Joseph impinged on later developments, especially insofar as the pope's speeches were concerned. Certainly, Saint Joseph must be venerated, but this must be done with respect for the discreet and strict ways that the evangelists use when referring to him.

I dare to propose a *radical* theology about Saint Joseph. *Radical* in the sense that I aim to put God at the *root* of everything and to meditate about issues to their end. When I speak of Saint Joseph I want to speak of God just as Christians understand God, that is, always as the Trinity of Father, Son, and Holy Spirit.

This God-Trinity has communicated itself in history. Within this radical perspective it is not sufficient to have the Son and the Holy Spirit with their distinct missions within humanity. This can generate, as it has generated, Christ-centrism (i.e., Christ is the center of everything) and even Christ-monism (i.e., only Christ is important). Or it can give origin to exacerbated charismatism, that is, it can give origin to a view centered in the Holy Spirit, an age of the Holy Spirit, which leaves behind the Son, the age of the Son, as happened in the thirteenth century with Joaquim de Fiore. Or it can create a community of charisma without any sort of organization. Or it can create a Christianity of sheer enthusiasm and of exaltation of religious experience, as is currently happening with Christianity worldwide, which is a Christianity far from the cross, from issues of justice for the poor and from the limitations of the human condition.

We need the presence of the three divine Persons among us, Father, Son, and Holy Spirit. The Father must be joined with the Son and the Holy Spirit. Otherwise, we are left as if floating in air, without a sense of origin and of the end of all mystery of revelation and of God's communication in history, which are represented in the Person of the Father.

SAINT JOSEPH HELPS US TO UNDERSTAND GOD FURTHER

In other words, I want to speak of God in connection with Saint Joseph, but I want to speak of the God of the Christian experience, which is always a Trinity, a communion, a relation, and an eternal inclusion of the Persons with one another.

My intended radical theology begins from this perspective. It is *radical* because it intends to go to the roots and it is *radical* because it aims to approach ultimate questions.

Let us now refer back to the central issue of this book: Saint Joseph is connected with two divine Persons. Firstly, he is connected with the Holy Spirit, who came upon his wife Mary and who overshadowed her (Luke 1:35; "'The Holy Spirit will come upon you, and the power of the Most High will overshadow you'") in such a way that Mary became pregnant with Jesus. Secondly, he is connected with the Son, who overshadowed the world and who became flesh in Jesus, son of Mary (John 1:14; "And the Word became flesh and dwelt among us, full of grace and truth; we have beheld his glory, glory as of the only Son from the Father"). Saint Joseph, as the theologians have spoken about him since the sixteenth century, entered into a hypostatic relation via Mary and Jesus. Let me explain the term hypostatic relation: a *hypostatic relation* is the relation through which Saint Joseph relates himself in a unique and singular manner with the two divine Persons (NB: *hypostase* is the root of the term hypostatic and means "person" in Greek and in official theology). Therefore, he has started to be part of the order, which is proper to the divine Persons. Without Joseph there is no concrete incarnation as the gospels bear witness.

Within this scenario the Father has been excluded. According to theologians, the Father was the one who sent the Son through the power of the Holy Spirit. However, the Father has remained as an unfathomable mystery within the immanent Trinity according to the common theological understanding.

Is this the only point that can be asserted regarding the Father? Does not God-Trinity reveal itself as it is, that is, as Trinity? Is it not appropriate for the Father to have a niche to communicate and reveal himself? Who better than Joseph, father of Jesus—the incarnate Son through the action of the Holy Spirit—to be the personification of the celestial Father? Yes, this thesis will be defended in this work. Similarly to the Son and to the Holy Spirit, the Father also overshadowed us in the person of Saint Joseph.

Don't we say that the intent of God is complete wisdom, supreme harmony, and complete coherence? This intent, because it is divine, has some supreme characteristics. Theology itself, whilst elaborating views, always seeks a coherent and harmonic spirit by articulating all truths among themselves and by demonstrating the connections between the truth of God, the truth of revelation, the truth of creation, and the truth of history.

Within this coherence and symphony I dare to assert that the whole Trinity has communicated itself, revealed itself, and definitely entered into our history. The Divine Family, in a specific moment of evolution, took the form of a human family. The Father personalised himself in

Joseph, the Son in Jesus, and the Holy Spirit in Mary. It is as if the whole universe prepared the conditions for this event of infinite goodness.

Thus, we have reached in this way the apex of coherence and supreme symphony: humanity, history, and cosmos in evolution are inserted in the Kingdom of the Trinity. There was a missing piece in the architecture of indescribable completeness: the personification of the Father in the figure of Joseph of Nazareth.

During the unfolding of this work and in its appropriate place I shall provide some anthropological and theological reflections that support this theological premise, for which I use the technical term *theologumenon* (i.e., "theological theory"). This is not official doctrine and it is neither found in catechisms nor in official documents of the Magisterium. It is, however, a sound theological hypothesis and the outcome of much creative theological research, which is, as I mentioned before, the effort of going further and further into the *profunda Dei*, into the depths of the mystery of God-Trinity.

OUT OF OBSCURITY AND INTO THE LIGHT

My theological boldness needs to avoid being arrogant. It is, however, the culmination of ideas that are a trend in works about Saint Joseph. My work here seeks to make this trend explicit and to meditate on it to its ultimate questions, until now these ultimate questions were left unanswered and this thesis was only implicit. My efforts here are connected to a trend of reflection on this subject that has been growing through the years. This trend has slowly left its state of obscurity and come into the light.

If we pay close attention we can note that there is a growing and continuous trend with regards to recovering Saint Joseph. Firstly, we have gone through a phase of unawareness, of unconsciousness, during the first centuries of Christianity when Saint Joseph was only referred to in connection with the childhood years of Jesus in the gospels. However, there has been no homily done about Saint Joseph, as it was done with Mary and with the baby Jesus himself.

It was only in the thirteenth century that Saint Joseph gained status through the work of medieval scholars, who noted his place in the mystery of salvation, and especially of incarnation. Thus, from the unconscious phase we reached the subconscious one.

The conscious phase itself emerged only in the sixteenth century with Isidorus de Isolano (ca. 1475–1530) who published the *Summa de donis Sancti Joseph* (Sum of the Gifts of Saint Joseph), the first systematic treatise on Saint Joseph. This text is the reference point for all other posterior treatises.

Full consciousness was only reached, however, through the well-known Jesuit theologian Francisco Suárez (1548–1617), a scholar in Salamanca, Spain. His commentary on the *De Mysteriis Vitae Christi* (The Mysteries of the Life of Christ) represents a qualitative leap, because it situated the mystery of Saint Joseph in the hypostatic order, the order that is proper to divine Persons. That is to say, Joseph is not only a just and virtuous man, the father of Jesus; rather, his presence and his mystery bear a strong relation to the mystery of the incarnation, and as such, and somehow, this makes him a participant in the mystery of incarnation. Suárez coined an expression that has never left theological language: "Joseph is ordained to the order of hypostatic union" (*pertinet ad unionem hypostaticam*). These events took place in the seventeenth century.

It took a further two centuries for another step to take place. This occurred at the end of the nineteenth century when various theologians, such as G. M. Piccirelli and L. Bellover, and during the twentieth century when theologians such as A. Michel, B. Llamera, and especially the Canadian-Brazilian theologian Paul-Eugène Charbonneau, founded and spread their views. Without a doubt the most convincing argument comes from Charbonneau in his PhD thesis at the University of Montreal, when he asserted with very rigorous theological debate that Saint Joseph belongs to the hypostatic order, and as such, he belongs to the divine order.

Within this understanding Saint Joseph is no longer seen only through his human side, as a husband and father, but also through his divine side, due to his relation with the second Person of the Holy Trinity that became incarnate in Jesus. This Jesus is the son of his wife Mary and the fruit of the Holy Spirit, but taken on by Joseph as his son with all the implications that fatherhood encompasses.

This idea of the hypostatic relation of Saint Joseph with the Son of God has become such a popular idea among theologians to the point that the Magisterium of the Church in its exhortation of Saint Joseph, *Redemptoris Custos* (1989) by Pope John Paul II, clearly says that in the mystery of incarnation God did not only take on the form of the reality of Jesus but "was also 'taken up' in Joseph's human fatherhood."[1]

We reached an even higher level of consciousness, or awareness, when André Doze, in his book *Joseph ombre du Père*, asserted that there is a singular relation between Joseph, the father of Jesus, and the celestial Father. The expression *ombre*, "shadow" in English, was chosen as it is associated with others, such as overshadow, cloud, and tabernacles, as I will later analyze further. In the Old Testament these expressions are associated with the overwhelming and strong presence of God amongst the children of Israel or in the Jerusalem temple. *Shadow* was never understood as a mere metaphor, but as an image that gives a real and ontological content to the presence of God. I argue that the celestial Father has this presence, strong and real, in Saint Joseph.

The last step in the development of this idea was taken by the Brazilian friar Adauto Schumaker, who worked for more than fifty years in the Amazonian part of the state of Maranhão. On Saint Joseph's day, March 19, 1987, he had an inspiration, which he put in writing and spread wherever it was possible, an inspiration that Saint Joseph is "the personification of the Father," just as Jesus is the personification of the Son and Mary of the Holy Spirit. With this statement we have reached the apex of this view.

My central aim here is to take these statements and to try to give them a rigorous theological framework that will allow us to say: Saint Joseph appears, without a doubt, as the personification of the Father.

It is not only the case that Saint Joseph's ministry (what he has done) belongs to the hypostatic order, as Suárez would have it, and it is not solely the case either that Saint Joseph is the "shadow" of the Father, as Doze has argued. Saint Joseph is the Father present, personalized, and historicised in his person, as Adauto Schumaker intuited and as I reaffirm.

We have come full circle now as the whole Trinity has assumed our human condition and dwells among us. The celestial Trinity of the Father, Son and Holy Spirit turned itself into the terrestrial trinity of Jesus, Mary, and Joseph. And I shall put forward later the view of the Holy Trinity as a Divine Family which, as such, personifies itself in the human family, in the family of Jesus, Mary, and Joseph.

---

1. John Paul II, *Redemptoris Custos*, n. 21.

In support of my thesis I shall seek the best arguments that have been put forward thus far, and at the same time, incorporate contributions made by different subjects, such as philosophical anthropology, the psychoanalytic tradition, and modern cosmology. My thesis shall place Saint Joseph within the framework of the truth of the Christian faith, it will offer good reasons for a more enduring piety, and as such, it will provide us with more reasons to praise and worship God, who so worthily dedicated itself in its entirety to us in the figures that encompass the terrestrial trinity, which is a historical reflection of the celestial Trinity.

Theology that was born out of praise returns anew to the same praise—now however, enriched with more reasons to rejoice and to bless.

2

Dissolving Misunderstandings and Clichés

The figure of Saint Joseph is surrounded by ambiguities. On the one hand he is the good Joseph, the husband of Mary and father of Jesus, the hard worker. He has a place in the hearts of the faithful. Millions and millions of people in Western culture, which today is globalized, are named Joseph. Hundreds of religious movements have Saint Joseph as their patron saint. Cities and towns, squares, streets, bridges, hospitals, schools, and especially churches are named after Saint Joseph. He is part of our cultural landscape, from the personal to the public.

On the other hand, Saint Joseph is the prototype of the person who is a supporting actor, quiet and anonymous, of whose life we know very little. Nobody knows who exactly his father and mother were, nor does anybody know his age at the time of his engagement and marriage to Mary, nor does anybody know the circumstances and the occasion of his death. He is a shadow, however a benevolent one.

Alongside the highly positive issues linked with his person there are also some accounts, clichés, and misunderstandings, which, since the first centuries of Christianity, especially due to the apocryphal works, have endured time and reached us.

However questionable these accounts are, they served to feed the imagination and, as such, gained form in painting, in the arts, and in literature. We are continuously confronted by the idyllic scenes of Christmas and of the nativity scenes, where the baby Jesus is put between a cow and a donkey and is flanked by Mary and Joseph, who are inclined over and revering the mystery of divine goodness. And similarly we see the old man holding baby Jesus in his arms, looking at him with care and amazement because he knows he is loaded with mystery.

But as I want to put forward a critical reflection, which is actual and a form of creative theology, I feel the need to clean up the terrain from the beginning. It is imperative therefore to disentangle preconceptions and to overcome clichés that have encrusted Christian imagination. This is similar to the process of cleaning one's own spectacles. We do not damage the lenses, but clean them so that through them we are able to see well. In the same way, I will make the most of the apocryphal writings, for they contain some truths, but I must also recognize their limits and the misunderstandings that can arise from them.

The various points I will touch on below will be further developed as this work unfolds. For now it will suffice to refer to them briefly as a way of setting the context for a detailed reflection.

JOSEPH—IS HE A MAN WITHOUT A WOMAN?

Firstly, I must deal with the issue of those who question Joseph's unique situation, and there are many who question his situation. They say: Joseph is a man without a woman, Mary a woman without a man, and Jesus a boy without a father.

In reply to this I must remind these critics that in the New Testament it is clearly stated that Joseph has a woman (cf. Matt 1:20, 24); he was first Mary's fiancé (cf. Matt 1:18; Luke 1:27) and then her husband (cf. Matt 1:16, 19). He was Mary's man, he was her only husband (cf. Matt 1:16, 18, 20, 24; Luke 1:27; 2:5).

Mary had a man, Joseph, her fiancé and husband (cf. Matt 1:16, 19). They lived together (cf. Matt 1:24) and went to live in Nazareth (cf. Matt 2:23).

Therefore, in spite of the virginal conception and the virginity of Mary being preserved (cf. Matt 1:18–25; Luke 1:26–38), the gospels are not reluctant in calling Joseph the husband of Mary and Mary the wife of Joseph (cf. Matt 1:16, 18–20; Luke 1:27).

The son of Mary also becomes the son of Joseph in virtue of the matrimonial lace that unites them. For this reason, the gospels recognize Jesus as the son of Joseph (cf. Luke 3:23; 4:22b; John 1:45; 6:42) or as the son of the carpenter (cf. Matt 13:55), of whom he learned a trade, since they also call him the carpenter.

They form a constituted family, which is present and united in its entirety at the occasion of the birth of Jesus; which felt the fears of mortal persecution by Herod who wanted to sacrifice all boys in the region of Bethlehem where Jesus was born; which underwent together the bitterness of their rushed escape to Egypt; which on their return from Egypt literally went to hide in Nazareth because Archelaus, son of Herod, reigned in Judea and was as bloodthirsty as his father and might still desire to kill baby Jesus.

In the little village of Nazareth, just as all pious parents, they perform the rites of purification, circumcision, and of presenting the child in the temple. They initiate their son in the holy festivals and become worried when the boy at the age of twelve fails to join the caravan on their return to Nazareth and remains in the Temple.

The fact that the pregnancy was mysterious, by the Holy Spirit and not by Joseph, is not an obstruction to the creation of a family. There are those who hold a poor and reductionist view of the concept of a family, that is to say, those who think about the family solely in terms of a couple's bedroom, as if sexuality is everything in family life. From a more encompassing point of view and by referring to all elements that compose life as a couple, by referring specially to the mutual commitment and to shared responsibility, Mary and Joseph form a real family. All their belongings are in common, in common also is their lifestyle, in common are their concerns, in common is their responsibility to educate their son.[1] Therefore, Joseph is not incidentally a father and nor is Mary a mother by accident.

IS THIS A FAMILY OF UNEQUALS?

A second issue I must deal with is the following: some point out that this is a strange family because the relations between its members are absolutely unequal. Mary is servant to the Lord (cf. Luke 1:38); Joseph is provider and reputed father (cf. Luke 3:23); and Jesus is the incarnation of the Word that is God (cf. John 1:14). Mary speaks and meditates, keeping things close to her heart; Jesus speaks, teaches and perform miracles; and Joseph stays quiet and only dreams. How are we to articulate these differences within the same family? Wouldn't this be a family whose reality is merely virtual?

1. See some interesting insights on this issue by Françoise Dolto, the well-known psychoanalist, in the chapter "La Sainte Famille," in Dolto and Séverin, *L'évangile au risque de la psychanalyse*.

In answering these questions I say that the gospels do not provide us with the basis for such eccentric claims. The gospels show a normal and united family. The gospels speak of parents that go to the Temple and that, as parents, get worried with the disappearance of their child. And lastly, the gospels also say that the boy was obedient to his parents (cf. Luke 2:51).

The thesis that I defend in this book avoids any form of unbalance because God, as Father, Son, and Holy Spirit and thus as Divine Family, is no longer an immanent Trinity and Family focused on its own ineffable mystery; it is rather a historical trinity and family, and as such it is connected to human existence and it is personified as the Father in Joseph, as the Son in Jesus, and as the Holy Spirit in Mary. In this way a perfect equilibrium is established. Each one of them, Joseph, Jesus, and Mary, is different, but all of them maintain an intimate and singular relation with each other, a relation within the hypostatic order of the divine Persons, as I shall discuss in more detail later. Each person of the human family personifies a Person of the Divine Family.

JOSEPH—IS HE AN OLD MAN AND A WIDOWER?

Some imagine Mary as a kind of religious woman who inhabits a convent of cloistered nuns. And within this view, Joseph becomes a kind of guardian and protector of Mary, rather than Mary's husband. Joseph becomes an old patriarch with white beard and hair holding baby Jesus in one arm and a bunch of lilies in the other so to symbolize his chastity.

The gospels do not support these images. They are the outcome of imagination, which are sometimes ridiculous; they are connected to the apocryphal gospels that represent the popular theology of the less-educated strata of Christians of the first centuries of our Common Era. I shall deal with this issue in more detail in chapter 5.

Mary appears in the gospels as a pious woman who says to the angel, "let it be to me" (Luke 1:38), and who feels humble in the face of God's offering. But at the same time Mary is a strong woman whose courageous speech in the *Magnificat* song could resemble a revolutionary proclamation in a political rally for the masses. She has the courage to say of God: "he has put down the mighty from their thrones and exalted those of low degrees; he has filled the hungry with good things, and the rich he has sent empty away" (Luke 1:52–53). Lastly, Mary is a woman who faced the murder of her child by Herod, and who, because of this, had to escape into exile facing all the dangers that such venture comprises.

Joseph faces slander when he takes Mary, his fiancée, already pregnant by the Holy Spirit. He has the courage of going against the norms and takes her to his house (cf. Matt 1:24). He takes on the proper role of a father who aids in the childbirth; who takes the initiative to flee to Egypt and who chooses the right moment to return; who, along with his wife, does that which all educating fathers did at the time with reference to religious obligations; who worries when his son disappears. All these issues have more to do with the father who is seriously engaged with his family mission than with someone who is a mere protector and a zealous provider.

With reference to the white beard and hair and to his age, the gospels do not provide any hint suggesting Joseph's age. The apocryphal books that emerged some three or four hundred years later invented Joseph's age. Let me explain the context within which these texts appeared. They emerged as an apologetic preoccupation in justifying the existence of the brothers and sisters of Jesus, as spoken of by the gospels, who according to these apocryphal books are the fruit of Joseph's first marriage; and they also emerged as a preoccupation in defending Mary's virginity, which is also testified to in the gospels.

Because of this perspective these writings relate that Joseph was a widower and an old man, a man whose extreme advanced age rendered him impotent, and as such he would not be a threat, even if he was tempted, to Mary's virginity. In the apocryphal book *The History of Joseph the Carpenter* it is written, as we shall see later, that Joseph married for the first time when he was forty years old. He lived with his first wife for about forty-nine years and they had sons and daughters together (the "brothers" and "sisters" of Jesus). It was only when he was ninety-three years old that he married Mary and they would have lived together for eighteen years. Adding all this together, we reach the conclusion that Joseph died when he was one hundred and eleven years old. Such ideas are only founded in the imagination, however pious this imagination is.

What we do know is that according to Jewish custom a man traditionally married at the age of eighteen, that is, a man started to cohabit with his wife at the age of eighteen. According to this tradition, Joseph was eighteen, perhaps a little younger, perhaps a little older, when he decided to live with Mary.

There is nothing that suggests that he was a widower and an old man. This assumption comes later with the apocryphal books for the reasons I stated above. Therefore, we should envisage Joseph as a young father between the ages of eighteen and twenty.[2] As I shall demonstrate later the expressions *brothers* and *sisters* did not necessarily have to be understood as we understand these expressions today, as brothers and sisters in blood. Within the Jewish understanding of extended family cousins and close relatives were called and understood to be brothers and sisters.

Luke and Matthew, the evangelists who narrate a little about the childhood of Jesus, do not mention anything about Joseph having died. What is certain is that Joseph did not appear beside Jesus at any moment of Jesus' public life, which started when Jesus was around thirty years old according to Saint Luke (cf. Luke 3:23). The last time Joseph appears is when Jesus was twelve years old (close to the adulthood age, which was thirteen at the time) and when Jesus went to the Temple in Jerusalem with his parents. It was on this occasion that Jesus stayed behind in Jerusalem whilst the caravan returned to Nazareth. Joseph and Mary found him and made their dissatisfaction known. After this event the figure of Saint Joseph completely disappears. It is assumed that he died around this time or soon after. The life expectancy of a Roman citizen or of a Jew at the time was approximately twenty-two. Joseph must have broken this common life expectancy barrier.

It is certain that Joseph was not at the foot of the cross as Mary, and other women, and John were. The fact that Jesus invested the evangelist John at the cross with the task of looking after Mary (cf. John 19:27) reveals that Joseph must have been dead by then.

WAS THERE LOVE BETWEEN JOSEPH AND MARY?

Some ask: Given the uniqueness of the relationship between Joseph and Mary, was there really love between them? A more detailed answer to this question will be given in the next chapter. Here I shall refer to the reflections of a Catholic philosopher, who is one of the most renowned of the twentieth century, namely Jean Guitton. In his book *La Vierge Marie* (The Virgin Mary) he writes very persuasively that:

2. See Ephraïm *Joseph, un Père pour le Nouveau Millénaire*. There it is suggested that Joseph was thirty years old at the time when Jesus visited the Temple and, as such, we can deduce from this that Joseph married Mary when he was eighteen.

Generally speaking, we are led to believe that Mary did not really love Joseph. Rather, that she found in him a protector, a sort
of shadow that covered other people's eyes from seeing what was
happening in her womb. Similarly, we are led to believe that Joseph
loved Mary just as a patriarch loved a child that was entrusted
upon him. If this is the case then, in fact, love had no place in their
lives. But I ask here: For what reason wouldn't Joseph love Mary?
Why would he not respond to Mary's love? Wouldn't Joseph also
feel the need for caress in the quiet afternoons when he came
back tired from work? Did he not respond to love with love? Yes,
Joseph experienced love in a form that is absolutely indescribable, strong as the mountain streams, tranquil and pleasant as a
serene lake, and with the freshness of the water from a crystal
clear fountain. The love of the man is molded by the love of the
woman, who as a skilful educator moderates his impulses so that
these impulses become care and tenderness, and this enables him
to give and receive. The love of Mary and Joseph in the house of
Nazareth is similar to the love of Adam and Eve in the terrestrial
paradise before the fall. At a given moment, in the first dawn of
the world, love between Adam and Eve appeared. The same also
occurred between Joseph and Mary.[3]

They saw themselves as human creatures, they did not see themselves
as demi-gods. Everything that is really human, such as love, affection,
tenderness, could have blossomed in them. We could imagine their conversations about the mystery that took place in Mary. And their curiosity
about it: What is the boy going to be like? Will he indeed be "set for
the fall and rising of many in Israel" or "a sign that is spoken against"
(Luke 2:34)? What does it mean that he will be Immanuel ("God with
us") and Jesus ("God that saves")? And they felt a mutual respect, they
felt involved in a story that they did not invent, a story that they had no
way of controlling. But it is was a story that, with blessing and reverence,
was welcomed by them, even if they did not understand all the details—a
story that served as the source of reflections and meditations for them, as
the evangelist Luke clearly avows (cf. Luke 2:51).

The perpetual virginity of Mary depends on its acceptance and on
the support by Joseph. This does not mean that there was no caring and
intimate relationship between them. Cardinal Léon-Joseph Suenens, one
of the central figures of the Second Vatican Council (1962-65) and a

3. Guitton, *La Vierge Marie*, 32–34.

prominent theologian, says, perhaps with a little too much exaltation, that:

> In the heart of this family of Nazareth there is a woman, Mary, and her husband, Joseph. Their union embodies the plenitude of terrestrial love. Mary loved Joseph as perhaps no other woman had loved him. Joseph was for her a source of constant happiness. Both loved each other completely and were in perfect synchrony with their call. To renounce having children after Jesus does not represent an obstacle to love, it rather elevates and strengths it . . . Mary reached this complete intimacy only with her husband Joseph. Joseph saw in Mary only a human creature, and as such he welcomed her. He came to know with her an intimacy without precedent, an intimacy of a love that is as large as the world.[4]

But let us be realistic here: the human condition involves some tensions within a relationship, minor arguments that occur against the background of our daily lives, and growth through trust. The same must have been true of the relationship between Joseph and Mary. If this was not the case then how could they improve their virtues and their relationship? The limitations of human fragility present us with opportunities for purification and for growth.

The understanding of the current dominant culture, which is poisoned by an extreme and commercial eroticism, can hardly grasp the statements given above regarding the loving relationship between Joseph and Mary. Our culture operates with a reductionist understanding of love and of the various forms of realizing love. It narrowly associates love with sexuality and with genitalia, and as such it is incapable of understanding a love that goes beyond this form of expression. And this understanding is not only with reference to Joseph and Mary but also with reference to elderly couples and also people who are deeply united at a spiritual level. In this way, our culture does not understand and misunderstands the kind of love between two people that expresses an indescribable human grandiosity and ethic, such as the love between Mary and Joseph.

At any rate, we can imagine the strength and the sweetness, the tenderness and the vigor that was shown by Joseph in respect of his son, Jesus. Joseph, as any other father, tenderly takes the child in his arms, brings the child closer to his face and gives him lots of kisses, then he

---

4. Suenens, "Saint Joseph et le renouveau familial."

speaks sweetly to the child and makes him go to sleep with careful and tender movements. When the child is a bit older, he puts the child on his shoulders, he plays with the child on the ground, and as a carpenter he makes toys that are proper to his culture: wood wagons, sheep, little bulls, and little cows. Every teenager needs a role model to emulate, a role model that provides strength and security; every teenager needs to experiment with limits and learn how to achieve goals, and at the same time, every teenager also needs love and tenderness. Joseph took on the psychic function of the Oedipus who embraces and welcomes as well as one who set limits, who gives meaning to authority and forces growth.

DOES IT MAKE SENSE TO SPEAK OF MARRIAGE BETWEEN MARY AND JOSEPH?

There are some who question and debate: If Mary was a virgin and conceived through the Holy Spirit, why didn't she continue to be alone and a virgin? Why did she marry Joseph?

Within Church tradition and theology this question has received special attention. We do not need to reproduce here all the arguments concerning this issue. It will suffice here to concentrate on three points that seem to have remained relevant.

Firstly, there is the issue of safeguarding Mary's honour, which is a topic discussed at length by two evangelists, Luke and Matthew. A virgin bride turning up pregnant brought problems to the families involved and to the groom. The law prescribed the *Libellus Repudii*, that is, the process of prosecution and punishment by means of the repudiation of the woman. Joseph shows himself to be just, honorable, and full of understanding of the mystery when he marries Mary and when he consequently brings her to his home. It is noteworthy here that Jesus' future reputation is also safeguarded, a reputation which could have been, as it was, attacked by claims that he was a child of fornication and an illegitimate child.

Secondly, Jesus required a life absolutely normal, a life similar to the life of other children of his time, a life within a family, connected to parents, cousins and grandparents, a life in which he grew and matured in the sight of other people and of God. The doctrine of the incarnation neither postulates a miracle nor does it postulate something extraordinary in the life of Jesus. For this very reason the early church wisely distanced itself from the apocryphal writings, which fill Jesus life with miracles and absurdities and things that are even unworthy of common decency. The miracle of incarnation only affirms that everything that is human with all the ambiguities that are part of human existence, which is full of contradictions and limited—and the gospels call this the flesh—is appropriated by God. It is appropriated by God in such a deep and intimate manner that it is appropriate to say that God cried, was breast fed, became frustrated, cheered himself up, loved, and at the end, died on the cross.

Moreover, today we know due to the sciences what humanity always intuitively knew: a child only develops properly in the middle of a regular family. There the child finds the feminine and the masculine, love and norm, limitless desire and the limit of reality, care and work, prayer and the daily struggle for life. The boy, the teenager, the young Jesus had to face up to all these different issues in order to grow normally. The narrative of his life provided by the four evangelists shows that his process of becoming an individual was successful. Jesus is someone who perfectly integrated the masculine and the feminine. In Jesus we find vigor and courage in putting forward his proposal, and at the same time, we find tenderness and love towards the people he encounters. Jesus called his father "dear dad" ('abba) because that was the way he felt about Joseph. Psychology teaches us that the experience of the father and of the mother serves as the basis for a proper experience of God. Taking his family experience as a basis, Jesus could call God "my dear dad" ('abba). And this describes God as possessing some characteristics that reveals God as a Mother, a merciful mother. God is hence a maternal Father or a paternal Mother.

Thirdly and lastly, there is a strictly theological reason for the marriage between Joseph and Mary, a reason which is only accessible through faith. It was important for Mary to wed Joseph so that they could constitute a family that would serve as the basis for the divine Family of the Father, Son, and Holy Spirit to enter into the terrestrial family of Jesus, Mary, and Joseph, and as such reveal the way God really is, in intimacy and essence. It was important that this platform was completely human and at the same time of divine initiative—thus the importance of the virginal conception of Jesus. Jesus is of a woman, with the same origins that we have, who was the outcome of fifteen billion years of the evolutionary process and of eight million years of humanization. He is of a virgin that did not know man. And she becomes pregnant by the Holy Spirit and the Holy Spirit starts a new creation through her. This is the divine side of the process. In Jesus we have the human and the divine united together in plenitude.

But Mary is a sole woman. She does not constitute a family. But she can be one of the three pillars of a family. It was appropriate that the Divine Family encountered a human family, which was previously established. It was for this reason that Mary became engaged and later married Joseph. The child is born. Here we have an established family, complete, perfectly human and completely divine: Jesus, Mary, and Joseph.

In my understanding, the Holy Spirit is personified in Mary at the moment in which she says "yes" to the angel. From that moment onwards the Word starts to take a human form in her womb and incarnates in Jesus. And the Father, who started the whole process, comes and encounters its personification in the groom and father, Joseph. The entire Divine Family descends and enters history. The human family welcomes and embraces this silent and humble entrance by the Divine Family in the human family.

The world transfigures. It reaches a sort of infinite plenitude. God as the communion of the Persons, as the Divine Family, leaves its own mysteriousness behind and enters the factual human history. God–Trinity–Family turns itself into God-communion of people and human family. The narrative has ended. Now we must await the ultimate manifestation of its meaning: the enthroning of the universe, of history, of the human family, of each family, of each person in the Kingdom of the Trinity and in the Divine Family.

This is the ultimate meaning of Joseph in the purpose of the mystery. Now a real theology about Joseph, the husband, the father, the artisan, the educator, can take place. Now Josephology really becomes theology, that is to say, it reflects on God and on Joseph, starting with God and in the light of God.

3

The Historical Joseph: Artisan, Father, Husband, and Educator

I want to be consistent here with regard to the theoretical avenues that are available to us when I analyze the figure of Saint Joseph. It is important never to isolate Saint Joseph from the web of relationships in which he concretely lived his life, such as within the family, with Mary and Jesus, and with the divine Persons who were hidden within this family. In this way the figure of Saint Joseph is not misrepresented; on the contrary, its relevance is recovered, especially the silent and anonymous aspect of his daily life, which is common to all families.

It is true that in the gospels there is not a single passage that deals exclusively with Joseph, as it happens with Elizabeth, John the Baptist, and Jesus himself. He always appears within the context of the family, because it is within the family, as a husband and father, that he finds his natural place. From him there is not a single word that has been passed on; we only have access to his dreams; neither do we have any specific data about him, about his birth or death. When Jesus started his public life at the age of approximately thirty years (cf. Luke 3:23), Joseph presumably had already died. Only the apocryphal writings, as I shall demonstrate later, speak of Saint Joseph's life and present us with very detailed, and sometimes fantastic, accounts of his death.

JOSEPH, THE ARTISAN-CARPENTER

Firstly, it is important to note that Joseph did not come from the world of the letters (scribes) or of the law (Pharisees), or of the bureaucracy of the state (tax collectors and Sadducees), or of the priestly (*kohanim*) or Levitic class of the temple. Neither does he belong to one of the pious groups (such as the Essenes, Zealotes, and Pharisees), and there were many in his time. He is a man of the countryside, of the little village of Nazareth, which is so tiny that is not even mentioned in the Old Testament.

He has a profession: he is an artisan-builder (*tektōn* in Greek, *naggar* in Hebrew, and *faber* in Latin), which is a generic noun used to designate people who work with wood (*faber lignarius*), stone (*faber murarius*) and metal (*faber ferrarius*).

Sources of the time give the understanding that a builder was essentially a carpenter who did houses, roofs, yokes, furniture, wheels, shelves, benches, wagons, oars, and masts; but who also knew how to work with stone, building houses, walls, graves, and terraces; and who could also handle metal and make hoes, shovels, nails, and gates.[1]

The builder-carpenter-artisan usually had his workshop in the courtyard of his house. There he stored the wood, the saw, the axe, the hammer, the nails, the wedges, the plumb line, the square, and the roll of string. Jesus was initiated in his professional life by his father Joseph. Jesus is known as the "son of the carpenter" (Matt 13:55) or simply as "the carpenter" (Mark 6:3).

It is very likely that Joseph and Jesus also worked on sites elsewhere. It is known that Herod ordered the reconstruction of the town of Sepphoris, which is very close to Nazareth, and which was an arms depot that was burned down and destroyed by the local population. All the artisans of the area were conscripted for the work (cf. Matt 20:1–6). There is no reason to imagine that Joseph and Jesus were not employed in such major works.

Moreover, nobody at the time lived off a sole profession. Normally everybody had some sort of connection with work in the fields, be it in the growth of fruits and vegetables, or in the herding of goats, sheep, or cattle. Through this kind of work the basic necessities of the household were supplied. Even today Galilee possesses some of the most fertile lands in the world. Apples, pears, grapes, almonds, walnuts, and blackberries

---

1. See for instance the data collected by Clodovis Boff, who researched a wide bibliography on the topic, in *O Cotidiano de Maria de Nazaré*. See also Foucher, *Notre Père, Joseph le Charpentier*, esp. 207–19, which deals with the geograhic and cultural aspects of Joseph; Deiss, *Joseph, Marie et Jésus*, 109–52; T. Stramare, *Vangelo dei Misteri della Vita Nascota di Gesù*; Daniel-Rops, *Daily Life in the Time of Jesus*; Theissen and Merz, *The Historical Jesus*; Jeremias, *Jerusalem in the Time of Jesus*; Aron, *Gli anni Oscuri di Gesù*; Chouraqui, *La Vie Quotidienne des Hommes de la Bible*; Clavel, *Jésus le Fils du Charpentier*; Martelet, *Joseph de Nazareth*, esp. 118–24; and Clavel, *Joseph, Fils de David*.

grow well there. Its olive and fig trees are particularly famous. And the vegetables, such as the lentils, broad beans, onions, and garlic are abundant. Well known are its pumpkins, eggplant, cucumbers, melons, and peppers, not to mention its greens, such as parsley, chicory and lettuce, or its spicy herbs such as cumin, oregano, saffron, and aniseed.

It is within this working context of callused hands, sweaty faces, daily tiredness, and quietness that the anonymous life of the worker Joseph unfolded. It is well noted in the Apostolic Exhortation *Redemptoris Custos* of John Paul II: "In the human growth of Jesus 'in wisdom, age and grace' the *virtue of industriousness* played a notable role since 'work is a human good' which 'transforms nature' and makes man 'in a sense, more human.'"[2]

JOSEPH, HUSBAND OF MARY

One of the few sure things that the evangelists tell us about Joseph is this: he was Mary's man and her only husband (cf. Matt 1:16–18, 20–24; Luke 1:27; 2:5). But before being her husband, and in accordance with the Jewish custom, he was her fiancé: "Mary had been betrothed to Joseph" (Matt 1:18, Luke 1:27). In fact the engagement had the same legal status as that of the marriage.

But during the engagement period, "before they came together" (Matt 1:18), that is to say, before they started to live under the same roof and at the same table, Mary was found to be pregnant. This fact caused great bewilderment in Mary and deep anguish in Joseph. The situation was clarified by the words of the angel (cf. Matt 1:20), and they got married. The texts start to speak, thus, of "her husband Joseph" (Matt 1:19) and of "your wife Mary" (Matt 1:20).

Since this is in fact a family, where husband and wife are brought together through marriage, let us see how a Jewish wedding party took place at the time. The ceremony is well known through the preserved literature on the subject and this will guide my analysis.

The bride ought to be at least eleven and the groom thirteen years old. But it was the norm to wait until they reached the age of eighteen. It was not how we do it nowadays where the couple arrange and decide on their own to get married. In the Judaism of the time of Jesus a marriage was an agreement between families. The woman did not marry; she was

2. John Paul II, *Redemptoris Custos*, n. 23.

given in marriage. The father of Joseph, who was called Jacob according to Matthew (cf. Matt 1:16) and who was called Heli according to Luke (cf. Luke 2:23)—and we do not know with certainty who he was—arranged with Joachim, father of Mary, the dowry to be paid in cloth and jewels, in domestic utensils, and perhaps even in some sort of property as a kind of security in the event of death.

As in any business transaction there was some sort of haggling. The father of the groom tried to lower the "price of the bride" and the father of the bride sought to exalt the maximum possible of her gifts as a woman, her virtues and domestic abilities.

The terms being agreed, the commitment to engagement follows. This possesses the same legal status of marriage. The engaged couple behave as if married but they do not live together as a couple. The groom must look after the bride, support her, dress her, and attend to her needs. The marital cohabitation only happens after the festivities, which last a whole week, or only three days in the case of poor families.

It is possible to imagine the situation loaded with mystery and bewilderment that this marriage must have brought to Joseph and Mary, since Joseph married a pregnant woman, whose son whom she carried in her womb was not his, but who appeared by the power of the Holy Spirit. This fact was possibly the object of long and discreet talks between Mary and Joseph. The relatives, even the closest ones, do not take part in this mystery, for the simple reason that they are unable to understand it.

The wedding ceremony (*nisuin*) followed this ritual: at the front of a musical ensemble the groom, festively dressed, goes to meet the bride with the help of some friends and brings her back to their future home.

The bride waits at home richly dressed and perfumed and surrounded by female friends. She wears a broad white tunic, a veil at the head that reaches her feet and gold sandals on her feet. The two groups, the groom's and the bride's, gather together and with singing and dancing the pair is conducted to their future home.

On arriving at their home, the ritual of exchanging nuptial promises is done under a small canopy (*huppah*). The rabbi presiding over the ceremony lifts a wine cup and recites the blessing: "Blessed art thou, O Lord, our God, King of the universe, who hast sanctified us with thy precepts, and has prohibited us matrimonial alliances with our near relations, and to refrain from betrothed ones, and hast permitted us marriage by means of the canopy and wedding pledge. Blessed art thou, O Lord, who sanctifiest thy people Israel, by the means of the canopy and wedding pledge."

The groom and bride drink from the wine cup. And soon after the groom places the wedding ring on the bride's wedding finger, and vice versa. The presiding rabbi then takes into his hands a second wine chalice and recites over it seven blessings, all linked to the grace of marriage. The groom and bride also drink from this second chalice. The presiding rabbi then pours the wine left onto the ground and breaks the chalice. The meaning of this act is the following: just as the broken chalice cannot be properly restored, in the same way a marriage can never be restored; and for this reason, it must never be broken and everything must be done so that it succeeds.

The ceremony finishes with the singing of Psalm 45, which is a love song:

> *My heart overflows with a goodly theme; . . .*
> *You are the fairest of the sons of men;*
> *grace is poured upon your lips . . .*
> *Hear, O daughter, consider, and incline your hear;*
> *forget your people and your father's house;*
> *and the king will desire your beauty.*
> *Since he is your lord, bow to him*

Thus the party starts with much joy, food, drinks (especially wine), music, and dancing that last well into the night. It is like this for seven days and seven nights for the families with more resources, or three days for the families with less means. Afterwards everybody returns to the routine of daily tasks and worries.

The evangelist Luke clearly says that Joseph, after getting married, traveled from Nazareth in Galilee (northern Israel) to Bethlehem in Judea (southern Israel) in order to enlist in the census that the emperor Caesar Augustus had ordered throughout the empire. He did this "with Mary, his betrothed, who was with child" (Luke 2:5; Matt 1:20). I shall deal later with the issue of Mary's pregnancy since this is an issue that much troubled Joseph and which concealed a mysterious purpose. For now let us concentrate on the issue of Joseph as a husband.

The importance of genealogical trees in the tradition of Jewish families is well known. It was a kind of personal identity card. Each person and each family knew from which tribe they belonged and who were their forefathers. Joseph was from the tribe of David, the king, the prophet, the poet, the singer, and warrior. And the background was defined by the paternal lineage. It is in this way that the evangelist Matthew traces (in a artificial way) the genealogical tree of Jesus through the line of Joseph by repeating in chorus thirty-nine times: Abraham the father of Jacob, Jacob the father of Isaac, Isaac the father of . . . etc. When he reaches the crucial point where he is supposed to say "Joseph father of Jesus," he says instead: "Jacob the father of Joseph the husband of Mary, of whom Jesus was born, who is called Christ" (Matt 1:16).

Why was there such a break introduced? The evangelist is forced into this situation because for him as well as for the whole of the early Christian community Mary was and remained virgin even after becoming a mother.

Just as a footnote or as an explicative appendix, Matthew clarifies the reasons for the introduction of such modification (cf. Matt 1:18–25). And he does so for two reasons. Firstly, it was done so that Joseph could impose his name over Jesus and thus safeguarding a paternity that was socially acceptable. When one imposes a name over someone else one turns oneself into this person's father, even if one is not this person's biological father. By doing this Joseph avoids gossiping that Jesus was an illegitimate child, the fruit of a rape or even adultery. Secondly, so that the Davidic descent of Jesus is guaranteed; for the theology of the first community the Messiah had to come from the descendents of David. Jesus was believed to be and announced as the Messiah and as such he had to guarantee a connection with David. This was done by Joseph, who was of Davidic lineage, when he imposed his name over Jesus.

What is important for us here is that the evangelist Matthew recognizes that Joseph is *husband* of Mary (cf. Matt 1:16). Later in the narrative, when Joseph "resolved to divorce her quietly" (Matt 1:19) because of her pregnancy, the angel assures him by saying, "do not fear to take Mary your wife" (Matt 1:20). At the end when the whole issue was clarified the narrative concludes that "he took his wife" (Matt 1:24). Therefore, they became a couple, they are husband and wife in reality.

For the whole of the early Christian community it was a certainty that Mary became pregnant when she was still virgin and engaged. There is no debate to be found about this subject in either the Gospel of Saint Matthew or in the Gospel of Saint Luke. For them the question was rather: How was this possible?

When Joseph realized that Mary was pregnant he had only two options, which are well discussed in the apocryphal writings. The first option was to denounce Mary publically as an adulteress as it is required by Mosaic law. Such procedure required a court lawsuit with evidence and witnesses. Along with the shame of the situation came the punishments prescribed by law. The other option, given that he had nothing to do with her pregnancy and thus the reason for his anguish, was to distance himself from Mary and leave the situation to come to light and to be resolved by their relatives or by Mary herself.

But, certainly, Joseph and Mary held long and detailed conversations in trying to understand a fact that was just as usual as it was mysterious. Mary, certainly, swears innocence and tells Joseph about the visit of the angel who announced: "you will conceive in your womb and bear a son" (Luke 1:31). She reassures that she herself became anguished and surprised by saying: "How can this be, since I have no husband?" (Luke 1:43). To which the angel replied: "The Holy Spirit will come upon you and the power of the Most High will overshadow you" (Luke 1:35).

Joseph could have taken Mary's account as an invented story in an attempt to escape the accusation of infidelity and adultery. But as Saint Matthew asserts, Joseph was a just man (Matt 1:19), and therefore he was someone who guided his life according to God and who always sought the correct action. He gave a vote of confidence to Mary.

However, there was still the issue of explaining the problem to their relatives and to the community. How to explain the bride's pregnancy? In small villages everybody knows everything about everyone, and Mary's state would not pass unnoticed. It is at this point that Joseph starts to think about leaving Mary, leaving her quietly so that no scandal would arise (cf. Matt 1:19). And it is also at this point that the heavens interceded and that the angel advised Joseph to take Mary as his legal wife and to take her to live with him (cf. Matt 1:24–25).

The situation is resolved insofar as its social aspect is concerned, but it creates a possible problem for Joseph: he could be accused of causing Mary's pregnancy whilst Mary was still his fiancée and a virgin. He would have broken the one-year law of engagement. The marriage would be done in a rush even with the public understanding that Joseph was a frivolous man. Or even, Mary's version of the events would be accepted by all, and everybody would be astonished in the face of such an unusual and mysterious event, and would be in the expectation of what such an event would mean. As religious and pious people they would bow to the unfathomable mysteries of God. We do not have a way of certifying if this later version prevailed. This later version goes beyond everything that a pious Jew could imagine and expect of God. To all intents, however, it is fair to say that Joseph took the risk and considered himself to be Mary's husband and the father of Jesus, his son.

Nonetheless, the rumor that Jesus could be an illegitimate child remained in some circles. In the Gospel of Mark we find an ironic question posed by the inhabitants of Nazareth, since nothing escapes the scrutinizing eye of the neighbors who note Mary's premature pregnancy: "Is not this the carpenter, the son of Mary . . . ?" (Mark 6:3). This amounts to saying: "This is the carpenter whose father we do not know." In John 8:41 the Pharisees, who Jesus accuses as not being of the children of Abraham, reply hatefully: "We were not born of fornication; we have one Father, even God." With this statement the Pharisees reveal the suspicion that Jesus was the child of an illicit relation.

These passages in the gospels are connected with an ancient Jewish understanding, according to which Mary's virginity stands for an attempt to occult the unspeakable origins of Jesus. Celsus, a second-century Greek philosopher, one of the major pagan intellectuals of the ancient world and fierce enemy of Christianity, accused Jesus of forging the story of the virginal birth in order to cover up his mother's adultery. Celsus says: "[Jesus was] born in a certain Jewish village, of a poor woman of the country, who gained her subsistence by spinning, and who was turned out of the house by her husband, a carpenter by trade, because she was convicted of adultery; that after being driven away by her husband, and wandering about for a time, she disgracefully gave birth to Jesus, an illegitimate child . . ."[3]

Celsus even cites the name of the Roman soldier who was presumed to be the father of Jesus, *Panther*. It seems to be a made up name as it works as an anagram of *parthenos*, which in Greek means "the son of a virgin." Son of a virgin, *huios parthenou*, gave origin to "Panther."

These cogitations were certainly elaborated by Christianity's adversaries, who sought to provide their version of the account of Mary's virginity and of the virginal conception of Jesus. At any rate, these cogitations are connected to an event that was witnessed by Luke and Matthew: Jesus is the son of a virgin, who was made pregnant by the Holy Spirit.

If we put this issue aside, we can put the following question forward: Since Joseph and Mary lived together as husband and wife, did they not

---

3. Quoted in Origen *Contra Celsum* 1.28.

love each other? did they not make love? Clodovis Boff, who studied this issue, answers:

> How would they not? They love each other as no other couple could. But their love is totally "absorbed" by the son, this son who was born in a way that was absolutely unusual and whose life was marked by a mysterious fate. Joseph and Mary were a "resolved couple." Thus, under the social image of a common couple, what happened in the recess of their home was totally anomalous for the cultural standards of the time. For these standards the woman is extremely characterized by her biology: she is 'womb' (cf. Judges 5:30), she is 'vessel' (cf. 1 Thessalonians 4:4). Her own virginity is a social as well as economic commodity. The hymen is the seal of the feminine honor. Nevertheless, with the couple of Nazareth, it happens differently: the woman acts as an active and free subject. It is not the woman who serves the husband, but the opposite: it is him who serves "his woman."[4]

JOSEPH, FATHER OF JESUS

The gospels present Jesus as "Joseph's son" (Luke 4:22), or as "Jesus of Nazareth, the son of Joseph" (John 1:45), or as "Jesus, the son of Joseph, whose father and mother we know?" (John 6:42), or as " the carpenter's son" (Matt 13:55), or as "the son (as was supposed) of Joseph" (Luke 3:23).

We know that Joseph was not a father in the genetic sense.[5] He is a father in the Semitic sense, a social father (he names the child and starts to live with Mary), he is a father in the matrimonial sense, and as I shall demonstrate below, he is a father in an absolutely unique sense. At any rate, Mary and Jesus are Joseph's family.

The crux of the question is how to qualify Joseph's fatherhood. The gospels do not provide us with further information or characterization. They simply say "Joseph, father of Jesus." But there is a need for some sort of characterization. Tradition has coined various characterizations, the majority of which are inadequate and some quite odd:

---

4. Clodovis Boff, *O cotidiano de Maria*, 63; see also the paper by Gauthier, "Der heilige Joseph in der Heilsgeschichte," 18–23, which contains various theologians' and spiritual writers' views on the issue of love and intimacy between Joseph and Mary.

5. See Grelot, "Saint Joseph."

- *Spiritual* father, which places him in opposition to carnal father, given that Jesus was not born of Joseph's semen. This title does not characterizes all the functions that a father assumes towards his children.

- *Davidic* father, because by imposing his name on Jesus, he inserts Jesus in the lineage of David, from which it was expected the Messiah would come. For us, nowadays, this title says very little since it is linked to a particular kind of Jewish theology.

- *Putative* father, because he is the reputed or supposed father. This is a totally exterior characterization and it does not do justice to the grandiosity of his mission alongside Jesus and Mary.

- *Legal* father, because he cohabits with Mary, Jesus' mother. Through this title Mary is spared from false suppositions and Jesus from spurious origins. However, just as the previous title, this is an extremely exterior characterization.

- *Adoptive* father, since he was not the natural father, he was father because he adopted Jesus as his son. In fact, what makes someone a father is not just the physical act of generation but his emotional, psychological, and moral commitment. It is this commitment that ascribes value and dignity to fatherhood. The father can even be absent from that whom he physically generated; but if he does not have this commitment then he is less a father than the adoptive father. Joseph seems to have held this view. He committed himself to everything that concerned Jesus and Mary. By naming the child "Jesus" he assumes the child and everything that this implicates in terms of commitment and duties.

- *Matrimonial* father: Joseph's fatherhood is the result of Joseph's marriage with Mary, a marriage that is real and legal. Joseph exercised all his rights and duties of father over Jesus. John Paul II, in his Apostolic Letter *Redemptoris Custos*, correctly says that Joseph's family is "a true human family . . . In this family Joseph is the father: his fatherhood is not . . . 'apparent' or merely 'substitute' . . . Rather, it is one that fully shares in authentic human fatherhood and the mission of a father in the family."[6] This characterization is perhaps the most objective and adequate.

6. John Paul II, *Redemptoris Custos*, n. 21.

- *Nurturing* father: Joseph is the father that nurtures and provides for the vital needs of his son; and this is something that Saint Joseph naturally did. This characterization, however, confuses a function of the father with the wider nature of fatherhood.

- *Functional* father, for he would he a father exterior to the family with the function of caring, nourishing, and educating; this would be some sort of responsibility which he was put in charge of by God.

- *Educating* father: Again this kind of characterization restricts itself to a function of fatherhood, however an important one. Here Joseph has the educating function of introducing Jesus to the cultural, religious and spiritual traditions of his people.

- *Virginal* father: This characterization answers the question concerning the sexual intimacy between Joseph and Mary. Since the time of the evangelists, tradition attests that Mary was always a virgin. She possessed a *virginitas uxorata* (virginity of a married woman), singular virginity that allowed her to be both a virgin and a mother at the same time. Such fact could only be possible as a divine deed, that is, Mary is mother not through the physical semen of Joseph but through the power of the Holy Spirit who preserved her virginity—and this was accepted by Joseph. Within this context it could be said that Joseph was a *virginal father*, an expression that will certainly be unpleasant to many people who cannot associate virginity with fatherhood. It would be better perhaps to use the expression *chaste father*. It is important to add here that the fortuitous virginity of Mary post-labor rested not only on her own personal choice, but also on Joseph's choice, who supported and accepted his wife's mission. Noteworthy here is that there is no dogmatic impediment if we accept that Joseph and Mary had a normal family life, just as any other couple, with sexual relations, with sons and daughters. Conjugal love is a symbol of God's covenant with humanity and with the church, as stated by Paul in his letter to the Ephesians (cf. Eph 5:29–33), and therefore it is a reality in which God is present. However, this was not the path chosen by God as witnessed in the gospels and by the Christian community since its early days.

- *Messianic* father: He was the father of he who was the Messiah, of Davidic origins. According to a prophecy of Isaiah (cf. 7:14) the Messiah would be born from a young virgin woman. By ascribing his Davidic genealogy upon Jesus, Joseph fulfills a requirement for the true Messiah; and Mary, being a virgin, fulfills the other requirement. *Messianic father* is an adequate title for the requirements of Jewish culture. However, it is a title that is somehow lacking since Jesus is more than a Messiah, he is the Son of God who became incarnate in our misery.

- *Personified* father: According to my *theologumenon* (i.e., theological theory) Joseph as a father (it does not matter under which title) allowed the heavenly Father to personify himself in him (Joseph), and as such the heavenly Father took the form of a concrete reality with all the functions that fatherhood involves. I will provide a detailed analysis of my theological reading later in this book.

All considered, it is clear that we are dealing with a kind of fatherhood that is singular and unique and which is lost within the mystery of God. God proposed to himself to assume human reality, and in this way he turns human reality into his own reality. God wanted to do this by following the path that is tread by all human beings, through the encounter and love between a man and a woman; in short, through the family, since everybody is born from a father and a mother, which normally are at the bosom of the family. It happens that the being who is being conceived and who is about to be born is not any human being. He is someone who, being perfect and completely human, participates in the Divine, comes from the bosom of God, is God himself. Here we find something singular, and if the fact is singular, then so too is the pathway. If this was the path chosen by God, that is, through a virgin woman, who is supported by her husband, who ended up accepting, after hesitating, his place in the pathway, then there is no reason for not respecting it with reverence and reflecting righteously upon the purpose that God desired to communicate.

To refer to a fact that is unique and that has no precedents one requires words that are also unique and unusual. But we lack such words, and we could not find them in any dictionary. How are we to overcome this problem? The Christian theological tradition has tried in a thousand ways to overcome this problem without success. All expressions are lacking in their attempt to capture the singularity of the fact.

Perhaps the most appropriate way of dealing with this issue is to restrict oneself to the language used by the holy texts and texts of the Christian tradition, which include the apocryphal writings, and simply say: *Joseph was and is father of Jesus of Nazareth*, and leave it until later for a proper reflection on an adequate understanding and appropriate terms about this fact.

THE BROTHERS AND SISTERS OF JESUS

A parallel question is the issue of the so-called "brothers and sisters of Jesus."[7] Mark and Matthew even cite the names of Jesus' brothers (James, Joseph, Simon, and Judas [cf. Mark 6:3; Matt 13:55]) and speak of sisters, without referring to their names, who live among them (cf. Mark 6:3; Matt 13:56). John tells us that "his brothers" urged Jesus to show himself in public, especially in Judea and in the capital Jerusalem (cf. John 7:3), but also states that "even his brothers did not believe in him [Jesus]" (John 7:5).

How are we to understand these brothers and sisters? Many historians, commenting without dogmatic references, understand that these brothers and sisters are real sons and daughters of Joseph and Mary. Within their view Jesus would be Joseph and Mary's youngest son or just one of their children. I restate what I have said previously: in dogmatic terms this is not impossible and it does not un-dignify God. A fecund marriage guarantees the perpetuity of human life. With the advent of more children Mary's reputation would increase, since for the Jews this would mean that Yahweh had blessed her. For the people of biblical times the sacred was maternity and not virginity or chaste purity.

But this is not in accord with the gospels that we have. They even hold Mary's virginity as a presupposition and refer to her surprise at the mysterious pregnancy. For this reason it is reasonable to remain in communion of faith with this tradition and with the Christian community, who have held this view and who continue to hold this view with respect to what happened to Mary.

Other historians and theologians put forward a hypothesis about the sons and daughters of Joseph as children of a marriage of Joseph anterior to his marriage to Mary. Joseph would, thus, be a widower and already

---

7. See Blinzler, *Die Brüder and Schwester Jesu*; Gächter, "Die Brüder Jesu"; Deiss, *Joseph, Marie, et Jésus*, 205–7; Algermissen, *Lexikon der Marienkunde*, 959–69; Lallement, *Mystère de la paternité de Saint Joseph*; Couture, *Saint Joseph Époux et Père*.

of a certain age, and he would have had married Mary later—and this is something that the apocryphal writings describe colorfully. The gospels, however, say nothing about this.

Others call attention to the fact that in the Old Testament the expression "brothers and sisters" does not necessarily mean "brothers and sisters" in the sense that we currently ascribe to these words. This expression could stand for "male and female cousins."

It is well known that in those days the concept of family was much more encompassing than the strictly nuclear concept of the family. For instance, it is said that Lot is brother of Abraham, but in reality Abraham was his uncle (Gen 13:8; 14:16); it is said that Jacob is brother of Laban, but Jacob was in fact his uncle (Gen 29:15); and Nadab and Abihu, who are sons of Aaron, are called brothers of Mishael and Elzaphan, who in reality are sons of an uncle of Aaron, namely Uzziel (cf. Lev 10:1–4).

If we take into account the concept of an extended family then we cannot conclude that the brothers and sisters of Jesus that Mark (cf. Mark 6:3) and Matthew (cf. Matt 13:55–56) make reference to are really sons and daughters of Joseph and Mary. On the contrary, there are some clues in the gospel tradition put together by John that indicate that Jesus is Mary's only child. After Jesus' death at the cross, because of the lack of siblings, Mary stayed at the house of the "disciple whom he [Jesus] loved" (John 19:26–27), she stayed in the care of John the Evangelist. This statement would be incomprehensible and at the same time strange if Mary had other sons and daughters who would naturally take care of her.

We can, however, affirm that Jesus was brought up within an extended family context with male and female cousins, who are considered relatives, who are Jesus' "brothers and sisters." They were so closely related but they were the first to misunderstand Jesus' activity as a wandering preacher in the villages of Galilee. In the Gospel of Mark, the oldest of the four gospels, which was written around the latter part of the fifth decade of our Common Era, it reads "they went out to seize him, for they said: 'He is beside himself'" (Mark 3:21). When they realize that Jesus has indeed left the house and started to systematically preach around Galilee, Mark says that "your [Jesus'] mother and your [Jesus'] brothers" went after him to speak to him and to bring him back home (Mark 3:21). It was at this point that Jesus made the necessary breakaway that marks the advent of a new period and of a new way for family connections, which is founded no longer in blood, but in faith and in the gospel. Jesus says:

"Whoever does the will of God is my brother, my sister, and my mother" (Mark 3:35).

JOSEPH, A JUST MAN

Saint Matthew characterizes the personality of Joseph by affirming that he was a "just" man (cf. Matt 1:19); the same thing is said of Simon by Saint Luke (cf. Luke 2:25).

What is the exact meaning of the word "just" within the Jewish understanding? Their understanding of "just" goes beyond our common modern understanding; when we say that someone is just we mean someone who ascribes an accurate worthiness to people and things, who acts righteously, who loves and observes the law. The biblical vision encompasses all these elements and others. There exists a true spirituality of the "just," and to understand this spirituality, we must combine two concepts: *ṣaddiq* (just) and *ḥasid* (pious).[8]

First comes the concept of pious *ḥasid*. The *ḥasid* is the person who lives intensely the duty to love God, who cultivates a great intimacy with him, who is sensitive to his intentions, which are expressed by the law as a live manifestation of his will. The pious person completely inserts himself or herself in the spiritual tradition of the people through a religious practice within the family, through taking part in the holy festivals, and through the weekly attendance of the synagogue.

The person who possesses this characteristic, who is pious, becomes just (*ṣaddiq*) when this person becomes a beacon of the community, educates the younger ones by example, conquers through acting righteously, and garners the trust of the rest of the community and thus becomes a reference for the collectivity. The life of the just shows true religious fervor and his or her integrity turns the just into a model of how to follow God. All these values are encompassed by the "just" within the Biblical understanding, and are the pathway for the just. The just is the one who is so much sung about in the Psalms in a chanting that starts with the very first psalm.

As one may gather, the "just" possess an important public mission. And for this reason, I cannot imagine, because of the characterization

---

8. See Spicq, "Joseph, son mari, étant juste (Mt 1, 19)"; Leal, "La misión de José en la historia de Jesús"; Sicari, "'Joseph justus' (Mt 1:19)"; Rasco, "El Anuncio a José"; and Ephraïm, *Joseph, un Père*, 18–23.

of Joseph as a silent and discreet figure that is found in the gospels, that Joseph was an anonymous figure lost in the masses. Even if he is characterized by silence because he was "just," his words bore weight, his advice was followed, his example of life was noticed. Saint Joseph is more than a mere artisan-carpenter with callused hands holding a saw, silent and reserved. Certainly, he is a manual worker, and as such, he is quiet, but we must not make him hostage of proletarian stereotypes. Rather, the workplace is where he earned his livelihood and also where he had the opportunity to experience God, to grow, silently, through meditating on the divine intentions. His love of God and his love of the neighbor, his observing of the traditions and of the law, all these constituted the aura that flooded his house and his workshop.

Such atmosphere was fundamental in Jesus education. If in his public life Jesus was able to show an unconditional love of God and to his neighbor, especially the little ones, to an extreme, it was because he had both learned this lesson in the school of Joseph and Mary, and especially because he saw their example. If he calls God 'Abba (Daddy), which is an expression of extreme intimacy, it is because he lived this intimacy with his father Joseph, who he also called 'Abba since he was a child, since this is the kind of term that children used towards their parents and grandparents.

JOSEPH, THE NAZARENE, THE SEVERINO

Joseph is a Nazarene, a citizen of the little village of Nazareth. The evangelists emphasize this fact. Why is Nazareth important as the place where the holy family lives? Firstly, it is important because it demonstrates that Joseph is in fact the father. In former times as it is in the present, it is normally within the competence of the father to decide the place where the family will live.

In fact, Saint Matthew says that Joseph "withdrew to the district of Galilee, and he went and dwelt in a city called Nazareth, that what was spoken by the prophets might be fulfilled, 'He shall be called a Nazarene'" (Matt 2:22–23).

Nazareth is not a proper city (*polis*), but a small village that is so insignificant that it demands the question: "Can anything good come out of Nazareth?" (John 1:46). It was there that Mary received the announcement of the conception of Jesus (cf. Luke 1:26–38). It was there that Jesus grew up and spent his young life (cf. Luke 2:39–52; Matt 2:23). From there Jesus left to preach in the villages around (cf. Matt 4:13; Mark 1:9) and thus started his public life, which was beforehand totally private and in the bosom of the family. He was even called for this reason the prophet of Nazareth (cf. Matt 4:13).

The first Christians were initially called Nazarenes, a term that was abandoned around the year 43 CE in Antioch when the Roman magistrates, who considered the followers of Jesus to be members of a Jewish sect, started to call these followers Christians (cf. Acts 11:26; 26:28, 1 Pet 4:16).

Secondly, Nazareth is important because of the mysterious meaning signed by Saint Matthew when he refers to what the prophets had said: Jesus "shall be called Nazarene" (Matt 2:23).

In fact, some passages of the gospels speak of Jesus of Nazareth (cf. Matt 21:11; Mark 1:9; John 1:45). Other passages speak of Jesus Nazarene (cf. Mark 1:24; 10:47; 14:67; 16:6; Luke 4:34; 24:19). It is interesting to note that some passages, which are more numerous, refer to Jesus *nazoraios*, which is an adjective of difficult translation and as such it is simply translated as "Jesus Nazarene" (cf. Matt 2:23; 26:71; Luke 18:37; John 18:5–7; 19:19; Acts 2:22; 3:6; 4:10; 6:14; 22:8; 24:5; 26:9).[9]

What is the significance of Jesus being called a Nazarene and its variant *nazoraios*? Certainly, it is not motivated just because of his evident geographical situation (i.e., a citizen of the village of Nazareth), but because of a precise theological reason. And I wish to deal with this issue now.

Prima facie, Matthew's reference to the prophets refers to Isaiah 42:6 and 49:6, which are passages that contain the Hebrew verb *neṣer*, from which the term "Nazarene" comes, and which means "messianic offspring" or "messianic remains." Jesus would thus be the Messiah and the representative of "the remainder of Israel" who had always remained faithful to God in all treacherous circumstances that the history of the people of Israel had witnessed. Jesus inserts himself in the continuity of the visceral faithfulness to God.

---

9. For a detailed discussion on this topic see R. Laurentin, *Les Évangiles de l'Enfance du Christ*, which contains a detailed bibliography, 331–32; see also Brändle, "Jesús Nazareno por que?"; and for a Christology that ascribes the term *severino* to Jesus see Goldstein, *Brasilianische Christologie*, especially the first chapter "Uma Vida Severina" (roughly in English: "A 'Severina' Life"), 11–37, and the chapter "Um Nazareno do Ceará" ("A Nazarene from Ceará"—Ceará being a state in the impoverished Northeast of Brazil), 106.

"Nazarene" can also evoke the terms *nazir* and nazirite, which in Hebrew means a man who has been consecrated by God, as in the case of the prophets (cf. Amos 2:11). These "nazirites" symbolized this calling of God through some kind of abstention, such as not drinking wine (cf. Judges 13:14) or not cutting the hair as in the case of Samson (cf. 1 Samuel 1:11). There was even a fraternity of nazarites, *Nazirim*, the *nazareato* or *nazireado*. With regards to Jesus, it is possible that Matthew probably wanted to insinuate that Jesus, as in the case of the prophets, had also been called by God to be the Messiah. Thus, Matthew used the geographical reference that Jesus was a Nazarene and gave it a prophetic and messianic meaning. To say that Jesus was a "Nazarene" is the same as saying "Jesus, the promised Messiah."

It is important, however, not to forget that when the evangelists refer to Jesus as the Messiah that they are referring to the Messiah that is servant-sufferer, to the Messiah that takes on the sins of the world, to the Messiah that was crucified. This understanding of the Messiah is completely different from the popular and theological understanding of the time, which expected a Messiah-king, a Messiah-political liberator who would free the Jews from the Roman occupation, and a Messiah-high priest who would invigorate the piety and the conduct of the people. To say that Jesus is a Messiah-Nazarene is equivalent to saying that Jesus is a Messiah-*severino*, that is a Messiah who assumes the severity of life and death, the life and death *severina*, the hard life of anonymous people, those anonymous people who are called in the Northeast of Brazil, *severinos*.

This subtle change in understanding was captured by the evangelist, thinker, and seminal theologian, Saint John the Evangelist. He also called Jesus the Nazarene in his gospel. As it is well known the evangelist John sought to accurately understand events and to interpret the messages that are present in the names and symbols in these events. The fact that John calls Jesus the Nazarene from the beginning signals a very particular theological purpose, which is connected to the mystery of incarnation.

For Saint John the incarnation implies that the Word assumes the human condition of "flesh" (cf. John 1:14), that is to say, a life of weakness, of scorn and of humiliation. In a word, a *severina* life, in the sense given to this word in the poem "Morte e vida severina" ("Death and life 'severina'") by the poet João Cabral de Melo Neto, as given previously.

By referring to the historic-geographical fact that Jesus was a Nazarene, one can infer that this fact is of theological importance: Jesus is connected to a place that is not considered important (cf. John 1:45–46; 6:42), a place where, according to the thinking of the time, simple people lived who did not know the law (cf. John 7:4), the unknown and anonymous people, who in the language of the poet are *severinos*, those poor and marginalized who do not attract the attention of anyone.

God, however, wanted to incarnate exactly in this situation the "Nazarene," that is, *severina*, the humble and contradictory. In other words, God revealed himself in Jesus not because Jesus is 'human', but because Jesus is "Nazarene," which is the same as saying because Jesus is poor, despised, simple, and unknown just as the *severinos* of history.

It was Joseph who, by deciding to go and live in Nazareth and become a "Nazarene" (in both senses of the word, namely, a citizen of Nazareth and a *severino*), created the conditions for God's incarnation in this low situation. Joseph, therefore, helped the Word to concretely incarnate itself in the *severina* situation of the time. And with this, God demonstrated the messianic privilege of the poor and of the *severinos*. According to human criteria the poor and the *severinos* do not count at all, they do no exist. But for God they count because from among them came the Savior, they are the historical body of the Messiah.

If Mary gave to Jesus the physical "flesh," it was Joseph who provided the "*severina* flesh," the historic-social condition of poverty, by deciding to live in Nazareth.

JOSEPH TAKES CARE OF THE FAMILY
IN THEIR EXILE AND WANDERINGS

The first sign of Joseph's fatherhood is the care that he demonstrated towards the pregnant Mary by receiving her in his house as his wife (cf. Matt 1:24). He demonstrated even more care when Joseph and Mary were on their way to Bethlehem at the time of the census and Mary started to feel the first pains of labor.[10] He sought a place in the local inns, but there were no vacancies available (cf. Luke 2:7). Hence, they sought shelter in a stable. The manger where the recent-born was laid was a cavity in the wall where the animals received their rations (cf. Luke 2:7).

Joseph showed particular concern and care when it became known to him that Herod had ordered the killing of all children that were less than two years old in a particular region of Judea where Bethlehem was

10. See a detailed discussion on this topic in Vischer, "Comment Arriva la Naissance de Jésus-Christ?"

situated and which is the place of the birth of Jesus. Herod's act aimed to eliminate any eventual pretender to being "king" of Davidic ancestry, such as in the case of Jesus. As the village and its surrounding areas did not have a population that exceeded a thousand people, it is thought that Herod's act applied to no more than twenty boys who were less than two years old.[11]

Herod was a particularly bloodthirsty monarch. His hands were stained with the blood of his predecessors, Antigone and Hyrcanus, and of their families and supporters. In the year 7 BCE he ordered the strangulation of two of his sons, Alexander and Aristobulus, and in the year 4 BCE he ordered the strangulation of another son, Antipater, for he feared that they would snatch the throne. All this occurred around the year of his death, 4 BCE, and which is exactly around the time in which Saint Matthew situates the massacre of the innocents, which provoked the famous phrase of Caesar Augustus in Rome: "It is better to be born a pig than a child of Herod." This is a play of words, for the word "pig" in Greek is *hus* and the word "son" is *huios*.

Within this scenario of fear and anguish Joseph had to show courage and a focused head: "And he rose and took the child and his mother by night, and departed to Egypt" (Matt 2:14).

The family experienced the exile, not in a friendly country but in a country where their forefathers had been enslaved, in Egypt. There were a number of negative connotations that were associated with this country and which are present throughout the Old Testament. We have no account of Joseph, Mary, and Jesus' life there in Egypt. But the exiled, in the past as nowadays, face the same sort of experiences: the uncertainty of whether they are welcomed or not, what to eat, where to live, what sort of job to do, when is it safe to return home.

Here the figure of father Joseph played an extremely important role. It was left to him to provide some sort of security, to make sure that the basic necessities were provided, to establish minimum ties based on solidarity and friendship with their unknown neighbors.

Saint Matthew tells us that the family stayed in Egypt until Herod's death (around the year 4 BCE; cf. Matt 2:15). According to the new dating of the Christian Era, which corrects the previous miscalculation, Jesus was born four years prior to 1 CE. If this is correct, therefore, the family

---

11. See data and discussion on sources in Laurentin, *Les Évangiles de l'Enfance du Christ*, 436–37.

must have remained in Egypt one year at most, afterwards it returned to Judea (cf. Matt 2:22). But then, Archelaus, son of Herod, occupied the throne and he was no less bloodthirsty than his father (cf. Matt 2:22; Luke 19:12–27), and as such he was a threat to Joseph's family.

Hence, Joseph decided to go and live in the province of Galilee, in the north, and hide in Nazareth, a peaceful and irrelevant place. There, another of Herod's sons governed, Herod Antipas, who was less cruel than his brother Archelaus, but who lived on parties and orgies. He fell in love with his sister-in-law Herodias, something that was denounced by a cousin of Jesus, John the Baptist, who ended up in prison (cf. Luke 7:18–28) and was then decapitated.

All these moves from one place to another are problematic and charged with preoccupation. There are things to be packed, those objects that are more fragile require care, and the furniture stays behind. Moreover, there is all the care towards the young child and the traumatized mother. They could fall ill during the voyage, they must eat and drink and have a place to stay overnight guaranteed. All these tasks are duties of the father Joseph, which he certainly assumed with courage and determination.

JOSEPH EDUCATES JESUS AND TEACHES HIM THE TRADITIONS

Joseph's family strictly followed the tradition. Eight days after the birth (Luke 2:21), Jesus was circumcised and given a name by Joseph, Jesus ("God saves"). Forty days after, according to what was prescribed in the law (cf. Luke 2:22–40), the parents took Jesus to the temple in Jerusalem to be consecrated to God. Normally, the family would offer a lamb as an offering. But the poor must content themselves with a couple of turtle-doves or two pigeons, as was the case with Joseph's family (cf. Luke 2:24). Afterwards they returned to their home in Nazareth, where they fell into the routine of common families who worked and lived with relatives and neighbors. The gospel says that "Jesus increased in wisdom and in stature, and in favor with God and man" (Luke 2:52).

Up to the age of five years old the child Jesus was particularly under the care of his mother. She allows him to play in the courtyard of their house and in the street; she leaves him to play with his cousins ("brothers" and "sisters") and friends. That which our greatest poet, Fernando Pessoa, has written about the child Jesus may be absolutely true:

And he's a natural child with a wonderful laugh.

He wipes his nose on his right arm,

He splashes around in the puddles,

He picks flowers and loves them and forgets them.

He throws stones at the donkeys,

He steals fruits from the orchards

And runs away from the dogs, screaming and yelling.[12]

The apocryphal writings, as I shall argue later, especially *The Infancy Gospel of Thomas*, provide accounts of the various mischief of the child Jesus, which caused his father Joseph to "pull his ears." Apart from that, Jesus helps his mother at home, he grinds the barley and the wheat in a mortar, he fetches firewood, he goes to fetch water from the spring, he crushes olives and collects up the fruits that are being sundried. He was obedient to his parents (cf. Luke 2:51).

After the age of five the father becomes the main figure. His mission is to help Jesus "be somebody." The scale of values is already determined by the law and by the prophets, which the boys learn about in the school of the synagogue from a very early age (Luke 4:17; John 8:6). At the age of thirteen he reaches adulthood, with religious maturity, and is considered a "son of the law." This is the end of his formal schooling. The rest of his education is provided by life and by the reading of the Scriptures at home and at the synagogue. That Jesus possessed a special vivacity is shown in the reaction of the Pharisees: "he has never studied" (John 7:15); and "who gave you this authority?" (Mark 11:28).

Joseph taught Jesus to pray. Father and son say the morning prayer early in the day turned to Jerusalem, where the sanctuary of God in the Temple is located. They give three steps forward to symbolize that they are placing themselves under the "sacred canopy" (*Shekinah*), where the divine presence converges.

They recite in a loud voice with eyes focused in the direction of Jerusalem: "Blessed art thou, O Lord our God, King of the world, the One Who forms light and Creator of darkness, Maker of peace and Creator of all things; who gives light in mercy to the earth and to those who live thereon, and in his goodness renews every day, continually, the work of creation. Let a new light shine over Zion and thy Messiah's light over us."[13]

12. Pessoa, *Keeper of Sheep*.

13. Translator's note: Boff refers here to the Jewish prayer *Yotzer*. I have used the

After this was said they say the famous proclamation of faith which starts with the words *Shemaʿ Israel* ("Hear, O Israel"), a creed that any Jewish person had on his or her lips and which the victims of the Nazi extermination camps recited aloud as they entered the gas chambers: "Hear, O Israel (*Shemaʿ Israel*), The Lord our God, the Lord is one; and you shall love the Lord your God with all your heart, and with all your soul . . . and with all your strength (Mark 12:29–30).

Afterwards they recite the six benedictions (some recite eighteen benedictions), which are repeated three times a day. I cite only the first and the last here:

> The first blessing: "Blessed are You, O Lord our God and God of our fathers, the God of Abraham, the God of Isaac and the God of Jacob, the great, the mighty and revered God, the Most High God who bestows loving kindnesses, the Creator of all, who recalls the good deeds of the fathers and who brings a Redeemer to their children's children for his name's sake, in love. O king, helper, savior and shield. Blessed are You, O Lord, the shield of Abraham."

> The last blessing: "Grant peace, goodness, blessing, grace, kindness, and compassion upon us and upon all of Your people Israel. Bless us, our Father, all of us as one, with the light of Your face, for with the light of Your face You gave to us, O God, the Torah of life and love of kindness, righteousness, blessing, compassion, life, and peace. And may it be good in Your eyes to bless Your people Israel at every time and at every hour with Your peace. Blessed art You, Lord, Who blesses His people Israel with peace."[14]

On Saturdays the entire family goes to the religious service at the synagogue: Joseph with Jesus at his front and Mary behind him as it was the custom in those days. Father and son sit in the central part of the synagogue, which was exclusively reserved for men, whilst Mary stays in the side or galleries above, which were allocated to the women. After reciting the Psalms and the blessings, they read passages from the Torah followed by extracts from the prophets. These passages were read by people who are chosen from among the participants. Joseph and Jesus must have

English translation available in Davies, *Christian Worship*, 15. Davies states this is probably one of the earliest versions of *Yotzer*.

14. Translator's note: Boff refers here to the Jewish *Schemoneh Esrei*, or *Amidah*, which is found in any Jewish Siddur.

taken part in these readings in turn. And after these readings a homily followed, which may be given by the coordinator or by someone who knows about theology or by one of the participants, as it happened on an occasion with Jesus in the synagogue of Nazareth, when he announced his program for liberation (Luke 4:17–22).

At the end, various prayers and the final blessing were said (cf. Num 6:24–26), which were later spread by Saint Francis: "The Lord bless you and keep you; The Lord make his face to shine upon you, and be gracious to you; The Lord lift up his countenance upon you, and be gracious to you." The rest of the day is spent with the spirit of sabbatical rest: not much walking, family life, and welcoming visitors.

Joseph introduced Jesus to all the traditions of the Jewish faith. And one of the main traditions of Judaism at the time was to visit Jerusalem yearly and celebrate the Passover (*Pesah*) in the Temple. The 140 kilometers that separated Nazareth from Jerusalem was traversed by caravans that were accompanied by joyful singing of the well-known "Psalms of Ascents" (cf. Pss 120–134).

The Temple of Jerusalem was one of the wonders of the ancient world; it sat in splendor on the top of Mount Zion. Its construction started in the year 20 BCE, which is around the same time as the birth of Mary, and it was inaugurated some ten years later but was only concluded in the year 63 CE. It was not only a religious place as it also performed other functions such as a law court, a college for rabbis, a bank, a market and citadel.

The pilgrims from Nazareth took the route via Bethany that reached Jerusalem in the Bezetha area. They went to the pool where the pilgrims purified themselves as well as washed the animals that were going to be sacrificed in the Temple.

When Jesus reached the age of twelve or thirteen, the age out which he would be considered an adult, he is taken to the Temple as Saint Luke narrates in some detail (cf. Luke 2:41–52). On this occasion the family goes to celebrate the Passover, which implies that they ate the Passover lamb and unleavened bread with bitter herbs accompanied by cups of wine (cf. Luke 22:14–18) and remembered the dangerous exit from Egypt, the land where their forefathers where enslaved (cf. Exod 12:15–20).

On the day before Passover (*Pesah*), in the afternoon of the fourteenth day of the month of Nisan ("April"), Joseph and Jesus take the lamb to the Temple to be sacrificed and bled on the altar by the hands of the priests of the Temple as it was demanded in the ritual arrangements given by Moses (cf. Exod 12:1–14). Only after this ritual is the lamb taken home and prepared by Mary and other women so that it can be eaten in the Passover meal (which was called *Haggadah* in ancient times and is called *Seder* nowadays). The celebrations last for seven days.

Afterwards, the grouping of joyful and noisy caravans start again so that pilgrims can return to their home towns. On this occasion, however, something that was not foreseen happened. Jesus stayed behind in Jerusalem as a lost boy. Joseph and Mary thought he had joined the caravan. They sought him among their relatives and acquaintances but they could not find him. They returned to Jerusalem and only found him three days after in the Temple in the middle of a heated debate with scholars, and this is something that provoked awe in everybody. His mother, bewildered, says: "Son, why have you treated us so? Behold, your father and I have been looking for you anxiously" (Luke 2:48). This is a just reprimand in the face of unacceptable behavior.

The field of Christology found an explanation for Jesus' behavior, who explains his actions on his own words: "How is it that you sought me? Did you not know that I must be in my Father's house?" (Luke 2:49). However, the text also says clearly that "they did not understand the saying which he spoke to them . . . and his mother kept all these things in her heart" (Luke 2:50–51). That said, Saint Luke also notes that Jesus went home with them and "was obedient to them" (Luke 2:51). With regards to the fact that Jesus was among the scholars in the Temple and debating with them, this fact ought to be understood within the context of the time. In the Temple talks were held all the time by scholars interested in the study of the Scriptures, and these talks were directed particularly to young people who, like Jesus, had reached the age of adulthood. Within this scenario Jesus' heated debate with the scholars and the awe it provoked in people is comprehensible.

Along with initiating Jesus in the piety and religious traditions of his people, Joseph also initiated Jesus in the profession of carpenter-artisan (cf. Matt 13:55). In his sermons, Jesus shows that he was well versed in this area as he speaks of wood, hay, and straw (1 Cor 3:12) and the house that was well built and the house that was badly built (cf. Matt 7:24–27; Luke 6:48–49). And because of his personal experiences as a worker he can say: "My Father is working still, and I am working" (John 5:17). The word "father" here can be either the heavenly Father and/or his terrestrial personification, Joseph of Nazareth, Jesus' father.

Finally, the primordial function of Joseph as a parent alongside Mary was to make the boy aware of all foundational experiences that mark life. If Jesus is whom we know, a courageous prophet, a wonderful story teller, a healer of many human diseases, a friend of the poor and excluded, someone who is full of tenderness towards children and women, and who is close to God, all these are greatly due to his parents, Mary and Joseph.

We do not require documents from the time to know the importance of mother and father in the first two to three formative years of the baby Jesus. Jean Piaget with his evolutive psychology and pedagogy, and especially D. W. Winnicott (with his pediatrics combined with childhood psychoanalysis) have provided us with a detailed account of the development of the human psyche during this initial and seminal stage of life.[15]

The primary maternal preoccupation, through which the mother identifies with the child, enables the mother to pass on the child the important feeling of safety, the feeling of being welcomed and not in danger. The child slowly starts to discover the other and starts to set himself or herself apart from the mother (the child holds fast to his or her comfort blanket or teddy bear, which Winnicott refers to as *transitional object*, and which the child does not let go of for anything in the world). This is the beginning of the discovery of otherness and also of the emergence of creativity, which enables the child to stay alone without being stressed but still connected to the mother. From this very moment the figure of the father starts to gain importance. The father strengthens the "I" of the child that is emerging and the child's self-assurance, which is the basis for one's loyalty to one's own convictions and to the truths that provide meaning to one's life. The idea of the other emerges more clearly as well as the limits that the other naturally poses. The emergence of the other before the child gives rise to the first ethical principle of inter-subjective relations, the principle of generosity and donation. The future ethical behavior of the child is fundamentally linked to this first occurrence of the other and to the responsibility towards the other. If Jesus in his public life showed himself as a being-for-the-others and gave a central role to loving thy neighbor, which he identifies as loving God (cf. Matt 22:39), it

15. See Winnicott, *The Child, the Family and the Outside World*; *The Family and Individual Development*; and *Talking to Parents*.

is because of his first experiences and contact with his father and mother, experiences and contacts that provide the foundations for the way he showed himself and for his views.

As we can gather, this subtle play in the relations between the mother-father-child builds a basic profile of the personality of the child for the rest of his or her life. Jesus underwent this schooling of feelings and emotions that were well developed and integrated, and this enables us to understand his singular personality, which is marked simultaneously by tenderness and vigor, by love towards others and by love towards God, by courage to tell the truth, and if needed by courage to break with tradition.

If Jesus transmits to us in his sermons the experience of God as 'Abba' (Daddy) it is because he previously lived this experience with his father Joseph. And according to my thesis, which I will argue in detail later, Joseph personifies the heavenly Father. Thus, it is perfectly normal that Jesus felt extremely close and intimate to God-Father since he experienced this close and intimate relation with his father Joseph.

JOSEPH'S DREAMS

Joseph did not receive any direct verbal communication, as did Mary. God and the angel (who appears in the name of God) communicate with Joseph exclusively through dreams: he must remain with Mary despite her pregnancy, name the child, escape to Egypt, return home and go to live in Nazareth (cf. Matt 1:20–21; 1:24; 2:13; 2:19–20).

There is much debate about the meaning of this form of divine communication through dreams.[16] For the whole ancient world (in Egypt, in Assyria, in Greece) dreams were the normal pathway for divine revelation. Socrates understood dreams as divine warnings, and in Homer dreams are considered to be messages of the gods.

In the Old Testament God sometimes reveals himself to the prophets through dreams (cf. Num 12:6; Dan 7:1; Joel 2:28) and other times these dreams are considered messages of God (cf. Gen 20:3; 28:12; 31:24; 1 Kgs 3:5). Moreover, the interpretation of dreams requires wisdom and skill.

It is interesting to note that within the theological tradition, such as within the tradition of Saint Thomas Aquinas, dreams were understood

16. The best study on this issue is the book by Resch, *Der Traum im Heilsplan Gottes.*

as a kind of inferior experience, as a kind of semi-life. The contributions of the modern deep psychology of Sigmund Freud and Carl Jung for an understanding of dreams and for the importance of dreams within the psychic totality of the human being were not known at the time.[17]

According to Freud and Jung, the conscious I comprehends only part of life. Beyond this conscious I there are the subconscious, the personal unconscious, and the collective unconscious. If words, metaphors, and concepts are the tolls of conscience, the dreams, the imaginary, the symbols, and the dreamlike figures are the expression of the unconscious. Through this language, which comes from the deepest levels of the psyche, emerges warnings, messages, compensations, and anticipations, which are connected to the process of individualization, and connected to the constitution of a mature and well-rounded personality.[18]

There are dreams and there are dreams. Some dreams are considered "great dreams" or "archetypal dreams" that are carriers of important messages that will guide the course of someone's life. Psychoanalysts warn us that it is important to pay attention to dreams, to analyze them, to let their meaning gradually unfold alongside life. The psychic totality mediated by dreams must be taken on so as to allow for a complete and more integrated human existence that goes beyond mere consciousness.

In theological terms we must say that when God reveals itself he enters into contact with the totality of human reality. Human reality encompasses the consciousness part, with words, concepts, and written messages that are understandable or possible to interpret, and it also encompasses the unconscious part with its rich symbolic capital that is expressed through the imaginary, through symbols and dreams. Hence, dreams are a form of divine revelation not only to prophets and the people of the Bible, such as Joel, Daniel, and our good Joseph, but also to us with our everyday dreams and/or our great dreams. One theologian who integrated the language of dreams in theological argumentation extremely well was John Sanford, who wrote extensively on the subject in *Dreams: God's Forgotten Language*.

17. See a very good explanation of the theory of dreams in Kelsey, *God, Dreams, and Revelation*. See also the following bibliography about dreams: Freud, *The Interpretation of Dreams*; Jung, *Symbols of Transformation*; *The Archetypes and the Collective Unconscious*; Edinger, *The Bible and the Psyche*; Tardan-Masquelier, *Jung*; Gallbach, *Learning from Dreams*.

18. See Jung's preface in White, *God and the Unconscious*; and also Jung, *Psychology and Religion*.

God communicated with Saint Joseph through the language of the depths. Perhaps this was the most adequate form of communication with Saint Joseph, who as a father represents the archetype of the origin, of the deepest mystery of which everything emanates. The important issue here is that Joseph understood his dreams as a calling alongside Mary and the child. In this way, Joseph fits into the supreme divine plan of God's self-communication as he is in himself, as he is Father (Joseph), Son (Jesus), and Holy Spirit (Mary).

JOSEPH'S SILENCE

An extremely puzzling issue is the veil of silence that covers the figure of Saint Joseph.[19] We know almost nothing about his biography. When Saint Matthew provides the genealogy of Saint Joseph he says that Saint Joseph's father was Jacob (cf. Matt 1:16). Saint Luke, however, says that Saint Joseph's father was Heli when he provides the genealogical tree that connects Jesus to Adam (cf. Luke 3:23). In other words, we do not exactly know who was Saint Joseph's father. We do not know his age when he married Mary, nor do we know his age at the time of death. Some reckon that he died soon after Jesus' official visit to the Temple in Jerusalem, when Jesus was around twelve, which is the age of maturity for a Jewish boy. Joseph had fulfilled his mission as "guardian of the Savior" around this time—as John Paul II says in the Apostolic Exhortation on Saint Joseph, the *Redemptoris Custos*—and therefore Joseph could leave the scene. This argument is very shallow and utilitarian. It turns Joseph into an unimportant actor within history, a history that he is not really part of; he becomes an extra.

Despite all these issues, the silence that completely surrounds the figure of Saint Joseph must not be an accident. Is there a secret meaning concerning this issue that must be identified? For me this is a task for theological reflection. Theological reflection does not want to inquire into this issue for mere curiosity; rather, it wants to discover through rational argumentation meanings that reveal the intentions of the Mystery. *Redemptoris Custos* rightly says:

> The aura of silence that envelops everything else about Joseph also shrouds his work as a carpenter in the house of Nazareth. It

19. Regarding the issue of silence, see Sanabria, "Le Mysterieux Silence de Saint Joseph"; Doze, "Marie révèle Joseph"; Siuta, "Saint Joseph et les Crises de la Vie."

is, however, a silence that reveals in a special way the inner portrait of the man. The Gospels speak exclusively of what Joseph "did." Still, they allow us to discover in his "actions"—shrouded in silence as they are—an aura of deep contemplation. Joseph was in daily contact with the mystery "hidden from ages past," and which "dwelt" under his roof.[20]

Here we find a plausible theological reflection. He, Saint Joseph, who came from silence was the one who first heard the Word. He, Jesus, who came from the obscurity of a common life was the one who first contemplated the light that illuminates every human being in the world (cf. John 1:9).

This silence is not the muteness of someone who has nothing to say. Joseph would have a lot to say. He, being a just man, in the sense I previously articulated, certainly shone more through his example than through his words. However, it is worth reminding the reader here that when things are too overwhelming we become quiet.

This silence is not the absence of one who is alienated and who does not realize what is happening either. Saint Joseph knows his mission, he reliably fulfills it and he is always present when he is required, such as during the period of pregnancy, during the child labor, in the choice of the name for the child, at circumcision, in the escape to Egypt, in the deciding moment of where to live, in the introduction of Jesus to the spiritual experiences of his people when Joseph accompanied Jesus to the Temple when Jesus was around twelve. And in all these, there is a plenitude of presence that is not well expressed through words, but through deeds and actions.

Paul Claudel, a great French writer and academic, was very interested in the figure of Saint Joseph especially because of his silence. In a letter to a friend, dated March 24, 1911, he writes: "The silence is the father of the Word. There in Nazareth are three people, who are very poor and who simply love each other. These are the ones who are going to change the face of the Earth."[21]

This love is lived in absolute silence, and it is indifferent to those who were considered important historical events of the time, be it in Jerusalem or in Rome.

20. John Paull II, *Redemptoris Custos*, n. 25
21. Claudel, "Letter."

Let me provide three fundamental reasons for understanding Joseph's silence as the most expressive and appropriate attitude for what he represents and for his significance to history and to the Christian community.

Firstly, Joseph's silence is the silence of all laborers. The speech of the laborer comes from his hands and not from his mouth. When we work, we become quiet, for we focus in what we are doing and in the object of our labor. Work belongs to the essence of the human being. Through work we mould ourselves. Given that nobody is born finished, but must rather complete the work that creation and the Creator have started. Through work we create a world that would never emerge through the forces of evolution alone, which are very complex and creative. Without a human being's work there could never emerge a house of wood or stone, the Holy Scriptures could never have been written, and the cars, the airplanes, and the rocket that took us to the moon could never have been invented. Work created all valuables in the world, and this was done during the silence of whoever was conceiving, in the silence of the hands that executed what was conceived.

Joseph's silence is inserted within this torrent of life and meaning that is represented by work. He who says "Joseph was a laborer, an artisan-carpenter" is closer to the truth than the one who says "Joseph was the protector of the Word of life," because he was protector of the Word of life whilst he was a laborer who with his work guaranteed the livelihood of the Life that is incarnated in our lives.

Secondly, Joseph's silence is the silence of the Father. The father Joseph represents the heavenly Father, and according to my understanding Saint Joseph is the personification of the eternal Father. The Father, who is in the heart of the Trinity, represents the nameless and speechless Mystery, the Principle of everything, the originating Fountain that generates every single thing. The eternal Father is inexpressible. Reason is speechless and the mouth is silent insofar as the eternal Father is concerned. He is the silence where all words originate. The one who speaks is the Word. He is intelligence, expression, and communication. The silence of the Father is hidden within each word and each sound of the universe. The silence reveals the essence of the heavenly Father. Joseph, who is the real and visible shadow of the Father, could only be and live in a silent way because in the contrary he would not be the personification of the heavenly Father. His silence reveals who he is: the eternal Father who is present and acting, who created the conditions for history to happen in the way that it did. Without Joseph, Mary would have been repudiated, she would not have had a home, the Word would not have entered a human family and would not have been protected when he was born in Bethlehem and would not have been defended when he had to go into exile. All these deeds were done in silence. Silence is the essence of Joseph and the essence of who he personifies, the heavenly Father.

Thirdly, Saint Joseph's silence expresses our daily lives and our interiority. Great parts of our lives unfold within the routine of our daily lives in the heart of our family and work. Certainly, there are conversations, sometimes even too much conversation. But when we want to hear the other we must be quiet. When we work we do not chat and we do not argue. Work is only well done and done with the necessary care when we are silent and when we concentrate on the task in hand.

All of us possess interiority. There is a universe of life, of emotion, of dreams, of archetypes, and of visions in our interior. From our interior we get voices and messages. These voices and messages advise us, warn us, and inspire us. Mingled with these voices and messages is the voice of God who calls us up for a more sincere life, more transparent, more open, and more pious. And we are only able to hear this voice and these voices if we become silent in our interior. The interior life is the life of the eloquent and fecund silence. It is in this silence that good intentions blossom, that dreams that give meaning to our expectations are elaborated, and that the words that transform reality originate.

Joseph is a master of the interior silent life. His silence is witness of another kind of holiness and grandiosity that is not expressed through the visual and through speeches. He is the patron of the vast majority of humankind who passes through this world unnoticed and anonymously, and who are often condemned to live in an iniquitous silence when they need to speak, protest, cry out against words that lie and actions that oppress. Joseph's silence shows the fecundity of non-speaking and of acting, of not expressing oneself and of being in the right place with presence and action.

This is the Joseph of history. He was a receptacle that was prepared to receive in his life the complete presence of the Father.

4

Saint Joseph of Faith: The Gospels

In the previous chapter I have focused mainly on data that is considered generally historical with reference to Mary, Jesus, and Joseph. This data is found within well-elaborated theological reflections by the two evangelists that make use of them, Saint Matthew and Saint Luke. The crucial point here is not to focus too much on the historical data per se, which is very sparse, but to focus on the manner in which this historical data is arranged and structured, which ascribes to this data a particular meaning that each of those evangelists wanted to communicate to their readers. This framing of the data is due to doctrinal and specific theological interests that are present in the reasoning of each of those evangelists.

THE THEOLOGY OF JESUS' CHILDHOOD

The two accounts of Jesus' childhood in which the figure of Saint Joseph appears are texts that were written late.[1] These accounts function as a kind of introduction to the Gospels, so to speak. They aim at placing Jesus, in one way or another, within the history of Israel, within the history of humankind, and even within the history of the universe.

I must emphasize here that theologically everything started with the resurrection of the Crucified.[2] The resurrection was the founding event

1. See a detailed discussion on the issue of exegesis connected to Jesus's childhood in Leonardo Boff, *Jesus Christ Liberator*; see also Laurentin, *Les Évangiles de l'Enfance du Christ*; Heising, *Gott wird Mensch*; Riedl, *Die Vorgeschichte Jesu*; Trilling, *Jesús y los Problemas de su Historicidad*, 85–97; Johnson, *The Purpose of the Biblical Genealogies*; Mersters, "Origem dos Quatro Evangelhos," 125–28.

2. For a detailed discussion on the importance of the resurrection for the Church and for theology see Leonardo Boff, *A Ressureição do Cristo e a Nossa na Morte*; Schnackenburg, "A Ressureição de Jesus Cristo como ponto Histórico da Fé em Cristo."

that opened up an absolutely amazing horizon for the apostles. If Jesus had not been resurrected then everything would have perished there and then. Jesus would have been one more prophet who filled the people with a hope of freedom, and who would have met a tragic end, just as it had happened with so many others before.

However, something unheard-of happened with this Crucified; suddenly women started to say: "The Lord has risen indeed" (Luke 24:34). This is the inaugural creed. Saint Paul in the Letter to the Romans, which was written in the year 57–58 CE says that Jesus was designated as Messiah and Son of God due to his resurrection (cf. Rom 1:4).

In the face of this unusual event, the apostles and disciples started very early on to question themselves: at which moment in the life of Jesus did God establish him as Messiah and Son of God? Saint Mark who wrote his Gospel around the years 67–69 CE answers: this was established at the time of Jesus' baptism by John the Baptist; in fact, Saint Mark's Gospel starts with this event and does not refer to Jesus' childhood at all.

Saint Matthew, who wrote his Gospel around the years 80–85 CE answers: Jesus is the awaited Messiah from birth and the ceremony in which Joseph imposed the name "Jesus" upon the child. Moreover, the entire history of the people of Israel, from Abraham on, led to this event, and for this reason, the evangelist constructs a genealogy that starts with Abraham and finishes with Joseph, Mary's husband and mother of Jesus (cf. Matt 1:1–17).

Saint Luke, who wrote his Gospel around the same time as Saint Matthew, goes further and answers: Jesus is the awaited Messiah and Son of God since the moment of his virginal conception. However, for Saint Luke, not only the history of the people of Israel but also the history of humanity as a whole since Adam led to this happening. It is for this reason that Saint Luke's genealogy starts with Jesus and refers back all the way to Adam, and from Adam it ends up with God (cf. Luke 3:38).

Lastly, Saint John, whose Gospel was written around the year 100 CE and, as such is influenced by an already mature theological reflection on Jesus answers: Jesus was Son of God even before the creation of the world because He was the Word and "in the beginning was the Word and the Word was with God" and "the Word became flesh and dwelt among us" in Jesus (John 1:1, 14).

Therefore, Jesus, Messiah and Son of God, is not only connected to the children of Abraham (Israel) but also to the children of Adam (humanity), and finally he is connected to the universe because "all things were made through him and without him was not anything made that was made" (John 1:3), and ultimately he is connected to God.

This is the background to the two evangelists' accounts of Jesus childhood in which the figure of Saint Joseph appears. The basic data is common to both evangelists: the virginal conception of Jesus, his birth in Bethlehem, his insertion into the Davidic line through Joseph, the escape to Egypt and the return and re-establishment of residence in Nazareth. This data is weaved through with theology and as such it is sometimes difficult to know what is conjecture and what is a real fact independent of conjecturing.

The intentions of Saint Matthew and Saint Luke were the following: How can one convince the Jews (Matthew) and the pagans (Luke) that Jesus was the awaited Messiah through the use of the facts that are available? What is the proof that we must provide to confirm that Jesus is without a doubt the Son of God?

The available facts must be arranged in such a way that they would yield convincing arguments. Thus, for instance, the Messiah had to be of David's lineage. How to attest to this if he is the son of the Virgin Mary who, by the fact that she is a woman, does not count for matters of lineage? The Messiah had to be born in Bethlehem. He is born there, but how to demonstrate that this was neither a fortuitous fact nor that Bethlehem is not a mere geographical place but that is has theological meaning? Certainly, according to the Scriptures the Messiah had to come from there.

The manner in which Saint Matthew argues is very different from the manner of Saint Luke.[3] Let me now demonstrate this difference.

The Perspective of Saint Matthew on Joseph

Saint Matthew's organization of the account of Jesus childhood starts with Joseph. He writes for Jews who converted to Christianity and who required some sort of convincing argument for themselves that was based in the Scriptures and in the prophets. With reference to the definition of Jesus' Davidic messiahship, the presence of Joseph was essential to demonstrating without a doubt that he was descended from David. And only he, as a man, could pass this lineage to Jesus. After overcoming his doubts

---

3. See a good introduction to this issue in Grelot, "Saint Joseph," 1290–93.

over Mary's pregnancy (cf. Matt 1:19–20), Joseph named the recent born child Jesus. With this gesture Joseph made himself father of Jesus, and as such Joseph connected Jesus to the genealogical line of David. This procedure was legally valid and recognized absolutely at the time.

After this Matthew refers to the order that Joseph receives in a dream to escape with the family to Egypt, and then, on his return to establish residence in Nazareth. Besides these points, a curtain of silence falls over the figure of Joseph. Nobody will ever know anything else about him.

The Perspective of Saint Luke on Joseph

Saint Luke writes the same account about Jesus childhood, but he starts with Mary. He probably inherited any information concerning Jesus' childhood and Joseph directly from Mary for he refers to her twice in his Gospel (cf. Luke 2:19, 51) or from the community of John the evangelist, because when John was at the foot of the cross Jesus asked John to take Mary under his care (cf. John 19:25–27). Saint Luke talks about Mary's engagement to Joseph (cf. Luke 1:27), about the journey from Nazareth to Bethlehem for the census (cf. Luke 2:4), and about how Joseph and Mary initiated Jesus in family rituals (circumcision, presentation at the Temple, and at the age of twelve the first official visit of Jesus to the Temple in Jerusalem).

Even if their theologies are different, both must be read for together they enrich our understanding of Joseph. Basically, the evangelists are not *directly* interested in Joseph because he did not pose a problem for the listeners of sermons. The problem was to present Jesus' messiahship. Thus, Joseph is the one who facilitated Jesus' insertion into the Davidic lineage. The focal point therefore is Jesus, not Joseph. But without Joseph, Jesus would not be the Christ, and that is to say, the Messiah of the Davidic tradition. Hence, the unquestionable importance of Joseph, which prevents him being totally ignored.

By taking into account the different concerns of each of the evangelists (for we do not face the same problems that they did) my theological reflection aims at developing things further. I intend to give a central role to Joseph and to show that in him something singular happened: the personification of the celestial Father. This celestial Father is the Father of the Son who was born of the Virgin Mary by the power of the Holy Spirit, and whom he named Jesus. This Holy Spirit overshadowed Mary (cf. Luke 1:35) and in this way Mary becomes pregnant by the Holy Spirit (cf. Matt 1:18). But it is through Joseph's fatherhood that the child Jesus is inserted into Jewish history, into human history, and into the history of the cosmos. Therefore, Joseph is vital.

My task now is to consider each of the theologies on Joseph, namely the theologies of the evangelist Matthew and of the evangelist Luke, and establish the extent to which these theologies can support my understanding of Joseph as the temporal *personification* of the eternal Father.

THE THEOLOGY OF SAINT LUKE ON JOSEPH

Saint Luke finds himself in a privileged position. He converted in Antioch, which alongside Alexandria in Egypt was one of the greatest city of the East, and he lives his faith in a community directly linked to Mary. Mary took refuge in this metropolis under the care of John. Saint Luke inherits directly from Mary or from the community the basic information concerning Jesus' childhood and Joseph.[4]

It is also important to say here that Luke has as a core experience, which orientates all his Gospel and his account of Jesus' childhood, not only the event of the resurrection but also the event of Pentecost. It is only Luke that refers to Pentecost in the Acts of the Apostles (cf. Acts 2:1–12). In Pentecost the new era of the Holy Spirit is inaugurated, for the Holy Spirit is poured out upon all flesh (cf. Acts 2:17) and it initiates the generation of a new being. This new being can only be the resurrected Jesus. It is for this reason that Luke is so preoccupied in his Gospel with demonstrating that he knows "all things accurately" and "from the beginning" (cf. Luke 1:1–3), for since the beginning Jesus is the fruit of the Holy Spirit's act.

In fact, the highest point of his account of the annunciation of the birth of Jesus (cf. Luke 1:26–38) is the absolutely crucial statement concerning Mary: "The Holy Spirit will come upon you, and the power of the Most High will overshadow you; therefore the child will be born will be called holy, the Son of God" (Luke 1:35).

Let me point out here that Luke uses the Greek verb *episkiasei*, which has been translated as "will overshadow you." The original sense in Greek is much stronger than this. For the Holy Spirit to come and "overshadow you" means that the Holy Spirit will permanently dwell in you, in Mary. In Hebrew "to dwell" and "to overshadow" is *shakan*, which is the root of

4. The most detailed study concerning this topic is found in Laurentin, *Les Évangiles de l'Enfance du Christ*, 13–397.

the word *shekinah*, which is a central concept in the Old Testament: the sacred canopy where God's presence converges in the Temple, the Holy of Holies, and amongst his people (Exod 25:8; 40:35; Num 35:34). This canopy-*shekinah* stands for the presence and for the permanent dwelling of God.

The *shekinah* is so important for Jewish theology that later it substitutes the Tetragrammaton YHWH (Yahweh, the name of God). In Greek *shekinah* is translated as *skene*. And to overshadow is *episkiasein*, which is the same verb used by Saint John to express the incarnation of the Word who dwelt amongst us (cf. John 1:14: *skenosen*).

Due to this point I have defended for many years the hypostatic relation between Mary and the Holy Spirit.[5] The textual evidence suggests a relation that is unique and exclusive between the Holy Spirit and Mary. The Holy Spirit, the third Person of the Holy Trinity, is the first to be sent to the world. He comes and turns Mary into his Temple (i.e., she is blessed among women; cf. Luke 1:42).

The first creation is attributed to the Spirit that moved over the face of the waters (cf. Gen 1:2). This creation, however, decayed. The new creation is equally the work of the Spirit. It begins with a woman, Mary. But with her the Spirit establishes a relation that is permanent and definitive (i.e., the spirit overshadows her). Only afterwards with his agreement, with his *fiat*, comes the Word, the second Person of the Holy Trinity, who grows in her womb.

Therefore, the Holy Spirit elevates Mary to his divine status. And from this divine status all that comes from her could only be divine and the Son of God. Only God can generate God. This is the reason Luke insightfully says, "therefore the child to be born will be called holy, the Son of God" (Luke 1:35).

The Hebrew language does not have the adjective *divine*. In its place it uses the adjective *holy*. Holy is the substantive specific to God, it is not a property among others, it is the very essence of God.[6] Thus, that which is born of Mary is "holy," as Saint Luke's text says, and as such, it has to do with the very essence of God. In other words, it is the "Son of God."

5. See a detailed discussion on this issue in Leonardo Boff, *The Maternal Face of God*, chap. 9. For exegetical details, see Laurentin, *Les Évangiles de l'Enfance du Christ*, 69–71, 198–99, 475–76.

6. See a discussion about "holy" in Laurentin, Les Évangiles de l'Enfance du Christ, 71, and especially n. 25.

If Saint Luke wished, at any given time, to put Mary at the center of the divine mystery then he could not have chosen a better way than by saying that the Holy Spirit came upon Mary. Here a crucial and insurmountable point was reached. It is so awe inspiring that even today it was not assimilated properly by the Christian churches and by official theology, who are hostages to the masculine perspective that greatly predominates in ecclesiastical circles. Without a doubt, Mary appears as the personification of the Holy Spirit, and it is in this way that the faithful experience her in the journey of faith, as in fact it was confirmed by the great psychoanalyst C. G. Jung in his research.

Joseph is not prima facie important at all. Luke only says that Joseph found Mary pregnant and took her to his home (cf. Luke 2:4–5). However, Joseph is fundamental for Luke's christological thesis since it is Joseph who inserts Jesus into the Davidic line, without which Jesus could not be the true Messiah.

According to prophecies in the Old Testament, the Messiah was expected at the end of the eleventh week of the world. Eleven weeks of the world are the same as seventy-seven days of the world. Saint Luke builds his genealogical account from Adam to Jesus, and shows that Jesus appears in the account exactly when seventy-seven days have been completed, with one day standing for each of Jesus' ancestors. Thus, the genealogy of Adam to Joseph encompasses seventy-seven ancestors (cf. Luke 3:23–38). History reached its apex when Jesus was born in Bethlehem as the ancient prophecies predicted (cf. Mic 5:2).

That Luke's account is artificial and ingeniously constructed is clear if we compare it to Matthew's account, since there is much divergence between them. Moreover, there are long time lapses between one generation and another. This is not really important. What Luke wants to indicate is this: everything converges in the new Adam, Jesus, since the beginning of humankind with the ancient Adam. Joseph participates in Mystery's plan by ascribing his Davidic origins to Jesus and assuming in this way Jesus' paternity.

Adding to this is the fact that the couple Joseph-Mary always appear together in all events in the account. Despite this Mary gains centrality in the account, such as in the case of Simeon's prophecy, which is directed to Mary: "Behold, this child is set for the fall and rise of many in Israel and for a sign that is spoken against" (Luke 2:34). And even when they find the child in the Temple it is Mary who speaks in the name of both parents and who complains to Jesus (cf. Luke 2:48).

Despite his secondary role, Joseph is twice called "father of Jesus" (cf. Luke 2:48; 3:23). Joseph takes on this paternity in all instances of the religious life of the family and up to the moment when Jesus starts preaching; and according to Luke, this took place when Jesus was roughly at the age of thirty and was supposed to be the son of Joseph (cf. Luke 3:23).

The Gospels say nothing about Jesus between the ages of twelve and thirty, nor do the Gospels say anything about his family during this period. There is only one very general statement regarding this: "And the child grew and became strong, filled with wisdom; and the favor of God was upon him" (Luke 2:40).

It is important to respect this silent period, which has theological importance as I shall demonstrate later. However, we are not totally uninformed about this period, as life itself with its daily routine is similar in all families and it is a source of understanding.

Detailed studies by Winicott, Piaget, and Vigotzki concerning child psychology and the progressive development of the human being reveal some very interesting data, which can be applied to the family of Joseph, Mary, and Jesus. These authors emphasize the importance of the first phase, the phase of mother-child relation, which is fundamental for the psychological well-being of the child. From the quality of this relation depends the feeling of safety, the sense of values and the adherence to one's own convictions and to one's own determination to pursue a project of life. The anonymous woman, who is amazed with Jesus and shouts from the middle of the crowd, is right when she says: "Blessed is the womb that bore you, and the breasts that you sucked" (Luke 11:27). Here is the evidence of Mary's educational work, without which Jesus would not have been who he was.

The father-child relation, a later phase, is equally important for the perception of the path to be followed, for the decision making process, to inspire courage so that difficulties can be faced and resolved, for an awareness of limits and for the experience of God. It is well-known that one's image of God is rooted in the image that one has of one's parents.

If Jesus established a new way of calling God by saying 'Abba ("my dear Daddy") it is because of the relation full of affection that he experienced with his father Joseph.[7]

We can imagine an earnest Jewish family full of piety tied up in their daily tasks but learning from their experiences and weaving their con-

---

7. A detailed discussion on *abba* is found in Leonardo Boff, *O Pai-Nosso*.

versations with religious topics and references. The evangelists' accounts reveal a family that is absolutely integrated into the religious tradition of the people. Jesus inherited this spirituality, which constitutes the empirical foundations for his preaching.

The happy father-child relation (a well-integrated Oedipus) is also shown in the fact that Jesus took on the profession of his father as he became an artisan. This presupposes a whole process of initiation, of apprenticeship, of an exchange of opinion and of working together. Within this interactive relation Jesus grew with his experiences, which constituted an opening to the world, to wisdom, to maturity, and to grace.

At a certain moment, however, the veil of consciousness is lifted from this "mysterious" child. In the event that happened in the Temple (cf. Luke 2:41–52) there is a sort of tension between the earthly father and the celestial Father: "Did you not know that I must be in my Father's house?" (Luke 2:49). The temple is the house of the Father (cf. John 2:16) and Jesus gives the understanding that his parents (Mary and Joseph) should have guessed this. Mary became aware of this fact for the evangelist says: "and his mother kept all these things in her heart" (Luke 2:51). Such events were the focus of much reflection by Mary and Joseph. Jesus was their beloved child, but he was also the Son of the celestial Father at the same time.

THE THEOLOGY OF SAINT MATTHEW ON JOSEPH

If for Luke the account of Jesus' childhood was centered around Mary, for Matthew it is Joseph who occupies this central focus. This is not because Matthew sees Joseph as the personification of the celestial Father; the evangelist Matthew does not go this far. Rather, Joseph occupies the centrality of Matthew's account for reasons connected with Matthew's own theology and for his preoccupation in proving to the Jews at the time that Jesus is a child of David, the awaited Messiah, and the new and definitive Moses. All these can only be proved if the figure of Joseph enters into the account. Otherwise, everything dissolves into thin air.[8]

8. The following texts are the essential bibliography on this topic: Stramare, *San Giuseppe nella S. Scrittura, nella teologia e nel culto*; Stramare, *Figlio di Giuseppe da Nazaret*; Stramare, "L'annunciazione a Giuseppe in Mt 1, 18–25"; Brown, "L'Annonce à Joseph"; Rochais, "La figure de Joseph."

For this reason in Matthew the annunciation of the birth of Jesus is done by an angel and in a dream to Joseph (cf. Matt 1:20), and not to Mary. We are very accustomed to the representation of the annunciation to Mary by the angel Gabriel as narrated by Luke (cf. Luke 1:26–38), which has been depicted by many artists throughout many centuries. Very rare are the representations of the annunciation that is also made to Joseph by an angel. This annunciation is as important as the one given to Mary. But since it was given in a dream, it is more difficult to be artistically represented, which contributed to the marginalization of the figure of Saint Joseph.

How then does Saint Joseph fit into Saint Matthew's theological understanding? Saint Matthew understands that it is a presupposition that cannot be doubted that Mary became pregnant by the Holy Spirit (cf. Matt 1:18), and this is a presupposition that is also present in the Gospel of Saint Luke (cf. Luke 1:35). The main concern of both evangelists was not to emphasize the virginal issue, but to emphasize the issue of Jesus' divine conception. For them the conception was virginal so that it could be divine, and not the other way round. For this reason the evangelists' texts prefer to speak of Mary as the mother of Jesus (cf. John 2:1, 3, 12; 19:25–26; Acts 1:14) and not simply as the virgin, which is something that only happens twice (cf. Luke 1:27; Matt 1:23).

Joseph is central in Saint Matthew's argument, since he wants to prove that Jesus is of David's lineage. If Jesus does not have Davidic ancestry then he is not the Messiah (cf. Matt 22:42). It is Joseph who provides the Davidic connection. As a contemporary commentator has correctly said, "In the society of those days, Jesus ran the risk of not truly being a person without Joseph. Mary furnished Jesus with biological existence; but it is Joseph who, by naming him, ascribed Jesus with social existence. Joseph gives Jesus roots in a people, in a lineage, in a tradition and in a profession that is socially acceptable."

Matthew makes use of theological resources that were considered valid at the time to reach the proof that Jesus was the Messiah and of Davidic lineage. Matthew takes the name David and through an extrapolation using numbers, and this is something that is common in the Jewish tradition and which was widely used later by the rabbis that forged the Talmud. The numerical calculation of the consonants of the name DaViD (the vowels do not count in Hebrew) results in the number 14 (i.e., D = 4 + V = 6 + D = 14). Following from this, Matthew builds Jesus' genealogy in such a way that it results in 3 times 14 generations, as he explicitly says (cf. 1:17). The number 14 is double the number 7, a number that in the Bible symbolizes the plenitude of God's realm or the totality of history.

The 14 generations between Abraham to David stand for the first important point in the history of Israel; the 14 generations between David until the deportation to Babylon reveal the lowest point in the history of the people; and the 14 generations from the Babylonian captivity to Christ stand for the highest point in history, a point which cannot be surpassed because in it the Messiah emerged.

I have mentioned previously that Matthew overcame the deadlock he faced in the genealogy, for when he reaches the end of the genealogy and says "Jacob the father of Joseph" the reader expects him to say "Joseph father of Jesus." But he does not. Matthew breaks his narrative in the list and affirms: "Jacob father of Joseph the husband of Mary, of whom Jesus was born, who is called the Christ" (Matt 1:16).

To solve the problem he faced, Matthew provides an account of the birth of Jesus that is centered on the figure of Joseph, who names the child Jesus. By naming the child Joseph becomes the legal father, and in this way he inserts Jesus into the Davidic lineage. Through Joseph Jesus becomes a child of David and as a child of David he is the true Messiah. Therefore, Isaiah's prophecy is fulfilled (cf. Isa 7:14), a prophecy according to which the Messiah would be born of an ʿalmah (a virgin or a young woman). God's plan is fully and completely accomplished.

As it happens, Joseph and Mary started to live together at the moment when Joseph discovers that Mary is pregnant. The fact that he thinks about breaking up the engagement (cf. Matt 1:19–20) reveals that Joseph was aware that the pregnancy had nothing to do with him. Joseph wanted to break up with Mary without exposing her to public shame, for it implied a process of culpable adultery (cf. Deut 22:20) or non-culpable adultery (e.g., as in the case of abuse or rape; cf. Deut 22:25–27). It is here that Matthew pays his biggest compliment to Joseph by saying that Joseph was "a just man" (Matt 1:19), and as such a virtuous man, a man who did everything in the light of God.

When the angel informed Joseph "that which is conceived in her is of the Holy Spirit" (Matt 1:20), he became reassured and "he took his wife" (Matt 1:24). Joseph opens himself to God's intention and he takes on the tasks of a father, as the Gospel narrates. According to Matthew it is fundamental that Joseph accepts God's intention that he be a husband

and father. On the one hand he saves Mary's reputation and on the other hand he inserts Jesus into the Davidic line.

The theological work of Matthew extends beyond the messianic identity of Jesus. Similar to Luke, who traces a parallel between John the Baptist and Jesus, Matthew also traces a parallel between Moses and Jesus.[9] It was a belief in the time in which the gospels were written (after the year 60 CE) that the Davidic Messiah was also a new Moses. They even used to say: "As it was with the first liberator, Moses, so it was also with the last one, the Messiah."

In fact, Matthew in his Gospel presents Jesus as a new Moses who, similar to the old Moses, provides a new law, the Sermon of the Mount (cf. Matt 5–7). The Jewish *midrash* of Moses (i.e., the midrash is the imaginative expansion of facts so that their meanings are clearer or better explained) narrates the following facts that allow Matthew to establish a parallel between Moses and Jesus: the pharaoh learns about the birth of Moses through the wise men, and in a similar way Herod learns about the birth of Jesus, the definitive Moses; the pharaoh and all his people became troubled, and so did Herod and all Jerusalem (cf. Matt 2:3); both the pharaoh and Herod order the killing of the innocents and, as in the case of Moses, Jesus escapes the killings; Moses' father learns in a dream that his son Moses will be the future liberator of his people, and Joseph in a similar way learns in a dream that Jesus "will save his people from their sins" (cf. Matt 1:21).

The parallels between Moses and Jesus are obvious and they are reinforced by the following passage in Exod 4:19–23, which says that after the death of the pharaoh "the Lord said to Moses in Midian, 'Go back to Egypt; for all the men who were seeking your life are dead.'" Moses takes his wife and son and returns to Egypt. Matthew 2:19–21 is the same, as after the death of Herod God speaks to Joseph in a dream: "Rise, take the child and his mother, and go to the land of Israel, for those who sought the child's life are dead." Joseph returns to Israel and goes to live in Nazareth. The destiny of the new Moses mirrors the destiny of the old Moses. As it was with the first so it was going to be with the last, the definitive.

The events that took place with Jesus at the time of Herod caused Matthew to establish a parallel with Moses and to see in Jesus God's in-

9. See Leonardo Boff, *Jesus Christ*, and the cited bibliography; Heising, *Gotts wird Mensch*, where the parallel between Moses and Jesus is discussed; Riedl, *Die Vorgeschichte Jesu*.

tention. Jesus is the true Messiah, the definitive liberator of his people, the Emmanuel, the God-with-us.

It has been demonstrated that the theology of Matthew explores to the maximum the figure of Joseph so that it can guarantee the messianic character of Jesus by inserting Jesus into the human family and into society through Joseph's naming of the child. God's incarnation requires this concretization, for if it was not so it would be just another version of the trans-cultural religious myth about the incarnation of deities.

COMMON ELEMENTS TO BOTH THEOLOGIES

Both theologians, Matthew and Luke, despite the differences in the elaboration of their accounts, make use of some fundamentally common elements.

Mary became pregnant by the Holy Spirit (cf. Matt 1:18–20; Luke 1:35) before she lived with Joseph or soon after they decided to live together.

Both evangelists affirm that an angel announced the birth and the name of the child Jesus and his destiny of being inserted into the Davidic line, and as such, of being the Messiah (cf. Matt 1:18–19; Luke 1:26–27, 32; and cf. also Rom 1:3 which says that Jesus "who was descended from David according to the flesh").

For both evangelists Mary is Joseph's wife (cf. Matt 1:20–24; Luke 2:5), and Joseph is Mary's husband (cf. Matt 1:16; Luke 2:48).

Luke and Matthew acknowledge the fact that Mary gave birth to Jesus at the time of Herod (cf. Matt 2:1; Luke 1:5) in Bethlehem (cf. Matt 2:5–8; Luke 2:4–5, 11).

For both of them Jesus is son of Joseph (cf. Luke 3:23; 4:22; Matt 1:21; John 1:45; 6:42), and Joseph is related to David (cf. Matt 1:16, 18, 20; Luke 1:27; 2:4) and he inserts the child into the Davidic lineage by naming the child (cf. Matt 1:21).

Both evangelists say that the family settles down in Nazareth (cf. Matt 2:23; Luke 2:39, 51; 4:16), which is an insignificant and poor place, where the three of them live together close to relatives in labor and in prayer.

Various theological themes are also common to them, such as for instance, that Jesus is a child of Abraham, a child of David through his father Joseph (cf. Matt 1:18–19; Luke 2:5), and that he is the Messiah-

Christ announced in the Scriptures. Both evangelists point out Jesus' divinity because he thought by the Holy Spirit. They emphasize the issue of universality, which is already present in the birth of Jesus (cf. Matt 2:1–2; Luke 2:31–32). And both sought resource in genealogies to insert Jesus into the history of Israel (since Abraham), into the history of humanity (since Adam), and into God (cf. Luke 3:37).

Such professions of faith are at the basis of my own profession of faith. Certainly, my way of arguing here is not the same since I do not share the same cultural references.[10] But I also, within my understanding of evolutionary cosmology, see the universe ascending, giving rise to complexities, increasing consciousness, and increasingly disclosing the Transcendent. We discover an infinite project and we are able to interact with the supreme Mystery. In Jesus the highest point is reached, for he awakens the clear consciousness of an intimate connection with God, who is experienced as 'Abba ("Dear Daddy"). To experience God as a dear daddy is to feel oneself to be a dear son.

Within the perspective of faith any and all disclosures of the conscience of the universe are directed to this: the deciphering of God, of the Emmanuel, that is present in us and that inhabits the cosmos, and to name and to venerate this God. Jesus is the first among many brothers and sisters (cf. Rom 8:29) who reached this new state of consciousness and who opened up the possibility for us to reach this God that is in us, and in doing so allow us to also say, "'Abba, Father" (Rom 8:15).

Joseph takes part in the complete revelation of God. He is close to Jesus, he is intimate with Mary, and he is directly connected to the celestial Father by the fact that he is also a father. Therefore, the conditions for a possible personification of the celestial Father in the terrestrial father have been established.

10. For good sources of current issues in Christology see Leonardo Boff, *Jesus Christ Liberator* and *Cry of the Poor Cry of the Earth*; Goldstein, *Brasilianische Christologie*; Moltmann, *The Way of Jesus Christ*; Segundo, *A História Perdida e Recuperada de Jesus de Nazaré*; Ferraro, *Cristologia*.

5

Saint Joseph of the Imaginary: The Apocryphal Writings

Those figures who are important for us and for our history are not always considered important in their own age. Jesus occupies without a doubt a central place in the history of humankind, in the history of the West and of the Christian churches. However, he was little noticed and seemed to hold little importance in his own age.

Besides Christian writings only a few sources refer to him, and these sources do so in passing. Flavius Josephus (born 37 CE), in his *The Judean Antiquities*, which has twenty "books," only makes two references to Jesus: one in which he mentions the martyrdom of James, "the brother of Jesus, who was called Christ," and another passage where he speaks of miracles and of the resurrection, which is a passage considered by commentators as a late addition to the text made under Christian influence.

Three Roman historians make small references to Christ. Suetonius (ca. 70–130 CE) in his *Lives of the Ceasars* refers to Christ in passing; Pliny the Younger, (63–ca. 113 CE), in his *Letter to Trajan*, speaks of hymns sang in honor of Christ as a God; Tacitus (ca. 56–117 CE) writing on the great fire that devastated Rome under Nero, says that this fire was allegedly caused by the *christiani*, who were the followers of someone called Jesus. This is all that we have from Roman historians.

With regards to Joseph we have even fewer references. If we depended on historical sources of the time we would not even know of his existence. The only sources that make reference to Saint Joseph are the gospels and the so-called apocryphal writings, which portray him in a very colorful way.

THE APOCRYPHAL WRITINGS: IMAGINING FAITH

Apocryphal writings (*apokruphos* in Greek means hidden or secret texts, because they are shared within the privacy of a group and are not used publically) are books, many of which are called gospels, such as the *Gospel of Peter*, the Coptic *Gospel of Thomas*, the *Gospel of the Hebrews*, the *Gospel of the Twelve*, the *Gospel of Mary Magdalene*, and others. They were written, by and large, during the second and third century of our Common Era. But they were not officially recognized as gospels by the early Church. The reason for this rests on the fact that these writings do not fulfill the minimum orthodox criteria that was developed through reflection by the early communities, within which we find the evangelists Mark, Matthew, Luke, and John.

If the gospels are the outcome of the intelligence of the faith (i.e., the gospels are the outcome of serious reflection and true theologies that underline the text), then the apocryphal writings are the outcome of the imaginary and popular belief. The apocryphal writings satisfy the legitimate curiosity of the faithful and fill in the gap of information in the gospels, especially with regards to those hidden years of the life of the family of Nazareth.

Moreover, many of these writings stand for the popular way of defending the Christian faith from attacks by heretics. Thus, for instance, when people started to discuss that Jesus was God, or only a prophet or a miracle worker, the apocryphal writings concerning Jesus' childhood were written. In these writings we find curious events that portray Jesus as having divine powers since the first moments of his life and childhood, as in the *Infancy Gospel of Thomas*.

In the *Infancy Gospel of Thomas*, for instance, whilst making sparrows out of clay with some friends, the ones made by Jesus filled themselves with life and flew away. Or a boy who was running brushed against Jesus and suddenly fell dead to the ground. Or another boy playing with Jesus on a roof fell and died and Jesus resurrected him. Or a son of Joseph, James, was bitten by a viper and was dying, and Jesus breathed over the wound and healed him, whilst the reptile broke apart.

Such imaginative narratives aimed at rebuking those who negated Jesus' divinity. And they attempted to present factual proofs of Jesus' divine nature by stating: "This child was either a God or an angel of God, for every word of his mouth is an accomplished deed."

When a rumor went around the Jewish community that Jesus was an illegitimate child of Mary, that Jesus was the result of a relation with a Roman soldier called Panther, the *Gospel of Philip* and the *Acts of Pilate* came to her defense and emphasized Mary's virginity and affirmed that Joseph was a good old man who was impotent and incapable of marital-sexual relations with Mary.

There was a time when no one paid any attention to the apocryphal writings because their narratives were too far-fetched. Despite this feature, the apocryphal writings inspired a great part of all the art produced under the auspices of the Church, of the little holy pictures that are given to children in Catholic countries, of illustrations in books, and of paintings and mosaics—particularly those of the great masters of the Renaissance; but they are also an inspiration in our modern times. The Holy Fathers, in their biblical commentaries and in their edifying sermons, made use of information available in the apocryphal writings. In this way these texts influenced popular piety, giving some color to the truths of the faith, which are generally embedded in theological language that is sometimes highly intellectualized.

When we believe, we believe with the totality of our being, with intellect, with emotion, and also with imagination. The apocryphal writings represent evangelization through the pathway of imagination; imagination possesses its own value and dignity for it is one of the ways in which humans express themselves.

Nowadays, commentators look at the apocryphal writings with a certain sympathy. They make use of modern methods of interpretation, which encompass assumptions from anthropology, from deep psychology, and from theories of the imagination, and this turns the apocryphal texts into fecund material for a kind of historical reconstruction of facts and situations of Jesus' time.

THE APOCRYPHAL WRITINGS ON JOSEPH

Just as I did with the gospels in the previous chapter, I want to do now with the seven apocryphal texts that make reference to Saint Joseph.

The Protoevangelium of James

This apocryphal writing is also known as the "History of the Birth of Mary." It is one of the most ancient apocryphal writings in our possession and it is believed to have been written at the end of the second century CE. It is attributed to James and for this reason it is also called *The Protoevangelium of James*. It was a very popular text in the Eastern Church and it only reached the Western Church in the sixteenth century CE when the French humanist Guillaume Postel (1510–1581) brought it from Constantinople.

The whole gospel is centered on Mary. Her conception is the fruit of prayers by Joachim and Anne, her parents, who were infertile. When Mary reaches the age of three she is interned in the temple where she is "nurtured like a dove [a symbol of purity] and received food from the hand of an angel" (*Prot. Jas.* 8:1). At the age of twelve, when she reaches the age of maturity for a Jewish woman, the high priest Zacharias convokes all the widowers of Judea. One of them will be her future husband following a sign from heaven. Each widower should bring a rod, and only Joseph's rod showed a sign: out of his rod a dove appeared and flew upon his head. Joseph received Mary into his home, but immediately becomes absent due to his work. When he returns after six months he finds Mary pregnant. Joseph faces a great personal crisis, which is well detailed in the narrative.

First, he reproaches himself because he received Mary as a virgin and did not protect her. Who had seduced her? Then, he reproaches Mary: "why have you humiliated your soul, you were brought up in the Holy of Holies and received food from the hand of an angel?" (*Prot. Jas.* 13:2). And Mary replies: "I am pure, and know not a man . . . As the Lord my God lives, I do not know whence it has come to me" (*Prot. Jas.* 13:3).

An impasse emerged for Joseph: if he hides Mary's fault, then he becomes her accomplice in sin and against the law of God; if he publicly denounces Mary as was the norm then he may incur an error and injustice, for what has taken place with Mary seems to be something mysterious and it may be of God. To escape this dilemma he opts to secretly repudiate her. Then an angel appears to him in a dream saying: "Do not fear this child. For that which is in her is of the Holy Spirit. She shall bear a son, and you shall call his name Jesus; for he shall save his people from their sins" (*Prot. Jas.* 14:2).

After this event, Mary and Joseph still faced other problems. A rumor went around saying that Joseph had furtively consummated his marriage and that he had taken Mary's virginity. When they are taken to a tribunal the both of them state their innocence. They are then submitted to a test, the so-called test of "the water of conviction of the Lord." Each of them is set apart from each other and then sent to the hill country. Some time after the both of them return in perfect health. The high priest thus states: "If the Lord God has not revealed your sins, neither do I judge you" (*Prot. Jas.* 16:2). Mary and Joseph return to their home overflowing with joy.

Then another problem emerges at the time of the census. Should Joseph present Mary as his wife or as his daughter? If he does present Mary as his wife then the problem of Mary's pregnancy arises again. And if he presents Mary as his daughter then he is stating something untrue. He leaves this issue to God.

During their trip to Bethlehem Mary enters labor. Joseph seeks a stable to safeguard Mary's decency and then goes after a midwife whilst his children look after Mary. Joseph says to the midwife that he received Mary as his wife; however, she was not really his wife because she conceived by the Holy Spirit.

And then to ascribe importance to the birth of Jesus a cosmic commotion takes place. Joseph, himself, is a witness of this event in one of the most beautiful texts of ancient Christianity, and this is something that was partly taken up by the Christmas liturgy of the Catholic Church. It is worth quoting a passage of this text here:

> Now I, Joseph, was walking, and yet I did not walk, and I looked up to the air and saw the air in amazement. And I looked up at the vault of heaven and saw it standing still and the birds of the heaven motionless . . . Those who chewed did not chew . . . and those who put something in their mouth put nothing in their mouth . . . And behold, sheep were being driven and they did not come forward but stood still; and the shepherd raised his hand to strike them with his staff but his hand remained upright. And I looked at the flow of the river, and saw the mouths of the kids over it and they did not drink. And then suddenly everything went on its course. (*Prot. Jas.* 18:2)

And with this the *Protoevangelium of James* interrupts its narrative on Joseph. It only states that once the child was born Joseph decided to go to Judea and to Jerusalem. The arrival of the three magi and the killing of the innocents are narrated without the presence of Joseph. The focus changes to Mary and to her cousin Elizabeth, whose son, John the Baptist, is being sought out to be killed, just as is Jesus.

This gospel is important for it shows the singularity of the relation between Joseph and Mary, as he is a widower and she is a virgin. Even if the Holy Spirit made her pregnant, she preserved her virginity.

The Infancy Gospel of Thomas

This apocryphal writing is divided into nineteen chapters and was written at the end of the second century CE, probably by a Hellenistic Christian who was not well-versed in the Hebrew language and literature, and it is fictitiously attributed to Thomas. It narrates Jesus' mischief, some of which are in such bad taste that they become almost scandalous.

Within a dogmatic perspective that understands Jesus to be the Son of God, this narrative frankly seems to be ridiculous, for it presents Jesus as cruel, arrogant, and cheeky towards his father and others, such as his schoolteachers. In this narrative Jesus is a real *enfant terrible*. But this apocryphal text falls within the tradition that Jesus has divine powers and that everything is under his control: he kills and resurrects, punishes and forgives. I have previously mentioned some of the events narrated in the *Infancy Gospel of Thomas* about the infancy of Jesus when he was six, eight, and twelve, and as such it is not necessary for me to repeat myself here.

Here, I am only interested in the figure of Joseph that appears in the ancient text. Joseph is always presented as the father of Jesus. Jesus himself calls Joseph a number of times as father. Joseph behaves as a true father as he worries about the future of his son Jesus. Joseph takes Jesus to school and repeatedly tries to find a teacher so that the child would not remain illiterate. But when Jesus meets his teachers he causes amazement, both at his wisdom, and also at his arrogance, which reaches the point of Jesus calling one of his teachers a hypocrite and humiliating him by saying, "You say what things you know, but I understand more things than you; for before the ages I am. And I know when your fathers' fathers were born, and I understand how many are the years of your life" (*Inf. Gos. Thom.* 6:2 [Greek text B]) Such events made Joseph irritated with Jesus. And on one occasion Joseph, as a fair father, "arose and took Him by the ear and pulled it violently" which provoked an explosive reaction from the child: "it is fitting for you to seek and not to find, and you have acted most unwisely. Do you not know that I am not yours? Do not vex me!" (*Inf. Gos. Thom.* 5:3). But Joseph fulfills his mission as a father and reprimands him. Joseph even said to Mary on one occasion, "do not let him go outside the door, for all those who provoke him die" (*Inf. Gos. Thom.* 14:3). And another time Joseph is filled with emotion as "he embraces the child and kisses him [Jesus] saying: Happy am I that God has given me this child" (*Inf. Gos. Thom.* 13:2).

On this occasion when Joseph was filled with emotion, Jesus was working alongside Joseph on some carpentry work. Jesus was helping Joseph to build a bed for a rich man. But as one of the beams was shorter than the other Jesus performed a miracle by elongating it to the size of the other. And in another instance, Jesus helps Joseph to sow wheat in a field. But that which was sowed by Jesus provided a much better harvest, and as such Jesus and Joseph distributed the fruits of this miraculous harvest amongst the poor afterwards.

This gospel finishes when Jesus is twelve in Jerusalem among wise men, and teaching these wise men in the same terms as narrated in the Gospel of Luke (cf. Luke 2:41–50). At the end it says that "Jesus . . . was subject to his parents," which contradicts what it said before, and "increased in wisdom and stature and grace" (*Inf. Gos. Thom.* 19:5). In truth, Joseph as father showed himself to be powerless in the face of the naughtiness and mischievous deeds of the child wherever he went. But Joseph never gave up on his educational mission of fatherhood, trying to impose his authority and limits.

The History of Joseph the Carpenter

This apocryphal writing is rich with information about the relationship between Joseph and Jesus. It was probably written in Egypt in either the fourth or fifth century CE in the Coptic language and it was later translated into Arabic. In fact, this text is a long narrative by Jesus on his father Joseph to the apostles on the Mount of Olives. Jesus starts by saying that he is going to narrate "the history of the death of our father, the holy old man, Joseph the Carpenter." This introduction to the text reveals the imaginative character of Jesus' speech. And thus, Jesus tells that Joseph was a carpenter from Bethlehem, a widower with six children: four sons (Judas, Justus, James, and Simon) and two daughters (Assia and Lydia). And he says: "But Joseph, that righteous man, my father after the flesh, and the spouse of my mother Mary" (*Hist. Jos. Carp.* 2). Jesus narrates Joseph's consternation when he finds Mary pregnant, and when Joseph thinks about secretly leaving her, and of the apparition of the angel to Joseph explaining that the child was conceived by the Holy Spirit. The text also tells us about the birth of Jesus in Bethlehem, and of the escape to Egypt and about the return to Galilee, which are events that we know about through the Gospels of Matthew and Luke. The text then says: "And Joseph, going back to his trade of a carpenter, earned his living by work of his hands; for, as the law of Moses had commanded, he never sought to live for nothing by another's labor" (*Hist. Jos. Carp.* 9).

And, contradicting the *Infancy Gospel of Thomas*, Jesus describes himself by saying:

> I moreover dwelt with them, not otherwise than if I had been one of his sons. But I passed all my life without fault. Mary I called my mother, and Joseph father, and I obeyed them in all that they said; nor did I ever contend against them, but complied with their commands, as other men whom earth produces are wont to do; nor did I at any time raise their anger or give any word or answer in opposition to them. On the contrary, I cherished them with great love, like the pupil of my eye. (*Hist. Jos. Carp.* 11)

Continuing with his narrative to the apostles, Jesus tells that Joseph married for the first time when he was forty years old and he remained married for forty-nine years when his wife died. Therefore he was eighty-nine years old when his wife died. He stayed as a widower for a year. Thereafter, from his engagement to Mary until the birth of Jesus three years had passed. Hence, Joseph was ninety-three at the time of Jesus' birth. He remained married to Mary for eighteen years. Taking all this into account, Joseph died at the age of one hundred and eleven.

Afterwards, Jesus narrated in a very detailed manner the death of his father Joseph. This apocryphal text in truth talks more about Joseph's death than about his life. Jesus says that, at a certain point, his father "loathed food and drink, and lost all his skill in his trade of carpentry" (*Hist. Jos. Carp.* 15–16). When death draws near Joseph expresses great sorrow and says eleven lamentations, in the same manner as Job, expressing contrition for eventual sins that he may have committed. This is the moment when Jesus enters the room and reveals himself to be the source of great comfort. Jesus says: "Hail! My father Joseph, thou righteous man; how is it with thee?" And Joseph answers: "All hail, my well-beloved son. Indeed, the agony and fear of death have already environed me; but as soon as I heard thy voice, my soul was at rest" (*Hist. Jos. Carp.* 17). After this Joseph makes a long speech remembering various events of his life with Mary and Jesus, and he even remembers the occasion when he "pulled His [Jesus] right ear, advising Him: to refrain from works that brought hatred upon Him," and "my son take care of thyself," and of Jesus' reply to Joseph when Jesus said, "art thou not my father after the flesh? I shall teach thee who I am." Then Joseph makes a profession of faith that is similar to the creed of the Christian community of the end of the second century CE: "Thou art my Lord, my God and Savior, most surely the Son of God" (*Hist. Jos. Carp.* 17).

Jesus then confides to the apostles: "When my father Joseph had thus spoken, he was unable to weep more. And I saw that death now had dominion over him" Lastly, Jesus describes the last moments of Joseph, his pains and agony: "And I was sitting at his feet looking at him, for the signs of death already appeared in his countenance . . . And I held his hands for a whole hour; and he turned his face to me, and made signs for me not to leave. Thereafter I put my hand upon his breast, and perceived his soul now near his throat, preparing to depart from its receptacle" (*Hist. Jos. Carp.* 19). And then Jesus describes death approaching with the ghosts that inhabit the mind of dying persons. Jesus had very pictorial visions of death and of the devil arriving with a host of servants "and their clothes, their faces, and their mouths poured forth flames." In the face of this macabre spectacle Joseph became very fearful and his eyes filled with tears. It is at this point that Jesus intervened: "when I saw the vehemence of his sighs, I drove back Death and all the host of servants which accompanied him." But death did not come quickly to Joseph and thus Jesus prayed strongly to the Father: "O Father of all mercy, eye that sees, and ear that hears, hearken to my prayers and supplications on behalf of the old man Joseph; . . . This is the hour in which my father has need of compassion." And then Jesus continues: "I reached forth my hand, and put right his eyes and shut his mouth" (*Hist. Jos. Carp.* 24). Joseph had just died.

And at the moment when Joseph is being buried, Jesus confides to the apostles that "I bewailed his death for a long time." Then Jesus took stock of Joseph's life: "And at the time when he fell asleep he had fulfilled a hundred and eleven years. Never did a tooth of his mouth hurt him, nor was his eyesight failed, nor his body bent, nor his strength impaired; but he worked at his trade of a carpenter to the very last day of his life" (*Hist. Jos. Carp.* 29). When Jesus finishes his narrative he leaves the following command, which served as an inspiration for me to write this book: "And thou hast ordered us to go into all the world and preach the holy gospel; and thou hast said: Relate to them the death of my father Joseph, and celebrate him with annual solemnity a festival and a sacred day" (*Hist. Jos. Carp.* 30).

To tell the truth, this commandment was forgotten by the Christian community, who for centuries left Saint Joseph in the shadows and at the margins of theological reflection. Only the popular tradition faithfully cultivated his memory.

Dialogues between Jesus, Mary, and Joseph

There is an apocryphal text of Ethiopian origins that is believed to have been written between the third and fourth centuries CE and deals with Mary's death. It is called the *Liber Requiei*. In the first part, an angel announces the nearing of Mary's death and Jesus recollects events from his childhood. Within this context the figure of Joseph emerges. Jesus remembers that as a boy he cried, "and Joseph was angry with you [Mary], saying: Give your breast to your child" (*Liber Req.* 5).

Later in the text Jesus remembers what Mary had said to Joseph during their escape to Egypt:

> "My Lord, we are hungry, and what do we have to eat in this desert place?" Then he rebuked you, saying, "What can I do for you? Is it not enough for you that I became a stranger to my family on your account; why didn't you guard your virginity, so that you would [not] be found in this; and not only you, but I and my children too; now I live here with you, and I do not even know what will happen to my seven children [. . .] There is no fruit that you could eat in the trees. This date-palm is tall, and I cannot climb it. I say to you that there is no one at all who has climbed, and there is nothing that a person will find in this desert. I have been afflicted from all sides because of you, because I have left my country. And I am afflicted because I did not know the child that you have; I only know that he is not from me. But I have thought in my heart, perhaps I had intercourse with you while drunk, and that I am even worse because I had determined to protect [you]. And behold, now it has been made known that I was not negligent, because there were [only] five months when I received you in [my] custody. And behold, this child is more than five months; for you embrace him with your hand. Truly, he was not from your seed, but from the Holy Spirit. And he will not leave you hungry,

but he will have mercy on you; he will provide me, and he will
remember that I am a sojourner, as you are a sojourner with me.
(*Liber Req.* 5–6)

And Jesus finishes his recollection by asking Mary: "Is this not everything
that Joseph said to you?" Then, Jesus the child turns to Joseph and says:
"My father, why don't you climb this date palm and bring it to her, so that
my mother might eat from it" (*Liber Req.* 7). Jesus, even as a child, ends
up performing a miracle: by his will the date-palm with fruits bends over
to the ground and thus his mother and father are able to eat.

Much later in the *Liber Requiei* the figure of Joseph reappears. This
happens when Mary tells some women about the troubles during their
escape to Egypt. Mary narrates the following:

When we were fleeing, Joseph, two of his children, and I, a ter-
ror was upon me, and I heard the voice of the infants behind me,
saying, "You do not weep and you do not lament; you see and you
do not see; you hear and you do not hear." And when it had said
this, I turned around to see who was speaking with me. And then
he had returned, and I did not know where he went. And I said to
Joseph, "Let us go from this place, because I saw an infant who is
not from this world." And then when I looked he appeared to me,
and I found that he was my son. (*Liber Req.* 41)

All the anguish of a family in need, escaping and fearful for its life becomes
clear and to the fore in this text. Moreover, Joseph's doubts about Mary's
mysterious pregnancy are recollected, doubts which are finally overcome
through Joseph's conviction that this pregnancy was something that had
been caused by the Holy Spirit.

Let me now refer to some apocryphal texts that were written much
later and which have little connection with theological literature, but
which nevertheless refer to some topics that are relevant for my reflections later in this book.

The Arabic Gospel of the Infancy of the Savior

This is an apocryphal text that was written much later, probably in the
sixth century CE, and which was written in Arabic. The oldest manuscript of this text, which contains illustrations, is a version of an older
Syriac text, and it was copied in the thirteenth century in Mardin, which
is located in the current Kurdistan region of Turkey.

I am not going to refer to this text in much detail, for it reiterates the narrative about Jesus' birth and childhood along the same lines as the *Infancy Gospel of Thomas*, which I have already referred to above. In this text Jesus appears as a child prodigy. When he was one year old and still in his cradle he says to his mother: "I am Jesus, the Son of God, the Logos, whom thou hast brought forth, as the angel Gabriel announced to thee; and my Father has sent me for the salvation of the world" (*Inf. of the Sav.* 1); which expresses the profession of faith of the Christian community of the first century CE. Jesus performs various miracles and is kinder, as he transforms his friends who have done something bad to him into goat-kids instead of annihilating them. In the debates with the wise men at the Temple he shows great knowledge of medicine, astronomy, and other sciences.

Jesus works with Joseph in carpentry and facilitates his work. When Joseph needed to cut, elongate, fit, or adapt anything, Jesus would just stretch his hands towards it and things were done. But we also see an inversion of roles in this text. It is Jesus who corrects Joseph and not the other way round as occurred in the *History of Joseph the Carpenter*. The *Arabic Gospel of the Infancy of the Savior* became well know particularly because of its narrative about the miracles that happened during the holy family's escape to Egypt (*Inf. of the Sav.* 9–26). When the holy family passed the trees bend over, and at the entrance of cities the land trembled and the idols fell from their altars to the floor (10). The bath water in which Jesus was washed cured leprosy (17, 18, 21), and the water used to wash his little clothes caused the appearance of fountains of bubbling water or sweet fruit trees (24). Jesus' clothes when placed over the head of a person freed this person from demons (11). Joseph, Mary, and Jesus came across thieves, but these thieves did not cause them any harm (13). One of these thieves, however, was the good thief who was later crucified alongside Jesus (23). Even a boy who had been transformed into a mule became human again when Jesus was placed over him (20).

Joseph appears as a good father who takes care of Jesus during their long journey through the desert and in Egypt.

The Gospel of Pseudo-Matthew

This is an apocryphal gospel that has been falsely attributed to the evangelist Matthew, thus the title *Pseudo-Matthew*, and it was written in the eighth century CE. It greatly influenced the arts and this can be seen in paintings by the Renaissance artists Fra Angelico and Raphael, and also later in paintings by Rubens and El Greco. This influence is due to the text portraying Jesus as a magical figure who works marvels with Mary's and Joseph's complicity. Hence, threatening dragons distance themselves after a simple look from the child Jesus (*Gos. Ps.-Matt.* 18). Lions and panthers peacefully accompany the oxen, asses, and beasts of burden that support the holy family, and they submissively wag their tales and show signs of adoration towards the child-God (19). A date palm bends over so that its fruits can be picked (20), and as a reward angels take a branch of this date palm to the heavens (21). The trip to Egypt does not last fifteen (or thirty) days as it does normally, but only one day (22). When the holy family enters a temple in Egypt, 365 idols fall to the ground and are completely destroyed (22). It is understandable that the artistic imagery of these narratives, which is absent in the Gospels of Luke and Matthew, has influenced popular religiosity, as well as literature and the arts even in modern times.

The Gospel of the Nativity of Mary

This apocryphal writing is the latest one, for it was written in the ninth century CE. It depicts an elderly Joseph (*Gos. Nat. Mary* 8), but not a widower, as is the case in the other apocryphal texts. When the choice amongst the elders was being made concerning who was going to be declared Mary's guardian a miracle happened: Joseph's rod is the only rod to blossom, and the Holy Spirit descends from the heavens and lands on it (8). Later this simple flower that blossomed in Joseph's rod becomes a lily, which is a sign of Joseph's purity. It is just like this that the representations of Joseph show him: on one arm he carries the child Jesus and in the other a bunch of white lilies.

In conclusion, the apocryphal writings entertain readers, excite the imagination, inspire the arts, feed popular piety, and provide answers to the natural curiosity of the faithful. These writings are, however, more legend than history. But due to their resonance in the concrete life of Christian communities, they help us to form a better picture of the figure of Saint Joseph by adding to his description in history and characterization in theology.

6

Saint Joseph of Reason: A Theological Reflection

For more than fifteen centuries the figure of Saint Joseph remained in obscurity and was ostracized by theologians.[1] With the exception of very recent times, Saint Joseph was never considered important enough to be subject of theological reflection, even for the popes in Rome.

It is enough to mention here that the Fathers of the Church have not written any homilies on Saint Joseph in either Greek or Latin. The first homilies and treatises on Saint Joseph started to appear only in the fifteenth century. It is of no consolation for us to know that Jacques-Bénigne Bossuet (1627–1704), the renowned French orator and pulpit preacher of the seventeenth century, rightly noted in his *Second Panégyrique de Saint Joseph* (Second Panegyric on Saint Joseph) on March 19, 1661: "l'Eglise n'a rien de plus illustre, parce qu'elle n'a rien de plus caché" (the most illustrious thing the Church has is that which she hides most).[2] This phrase comes across as an excuse for the hiding of Saint Joseph because of a lack of theological concern, due to a theology that was not creative enough and did not dare to go beyond the silence of the New Testament's texts about him.

But this does not imply that Saint Joseph was forgotten. It was in the heart of the common people that devotion to Saint Joseph took refuge, and from there it slowly gained ground in academic centers of theology and in official theology.

---

1. The well-known *Dictionary of Biblical Theology* by Xavier Léon-Dufour does not even have an entry on Saint Joseph, even though it does have entries for Mary and Jesus. It is interesting to note, however, that some years before the publication of the *Dictionary* Xavier Léon-Dufour wrote a very good paper on Saint Joseph: "L'Announce à Joseph."

2. Bossuet, *Oeuvres de Bossuet*, 3:429.

Let me provide here a very brief historical account of the Christian understanding on Saint Joseph and demonstrate how nowadays Saint Joseph starts to gain increasingly more relevance within a foundational theological perspective.[3]

SAINT JOSEPH IN THE HISTORY OF THEOLOGICAL IDEAS

In the first centuries of our Common Era Saint Joseph is incidentally present in the Christian consciousness, in the texts of the Fathers of the Church who commented on the gospel pericopes of Luke and Matthew on Jesus' childhood. Saint Hilary (301–367 CE), Saint Ambrose (ca 338–397 CE) and later Saint Bede (673–735 CE) wrote a little on Saint Joseph. The fact that Joseph was an artisan often reminds them of the celestial Father, the artisan of all things.

The main elements about Saint Joseph had already appeared by the fifth century CE. Later these elements provided the fundamentals for a more detailed theological reflection on Saint Joseph. These elements are: Joseph has a place within the history of salvation, he is at the service of Mary and Jesus; he is a just man, the chaste husband of Mary, the father of Jesus, and an example for a pious and hardworking life.

From the fifth century to the twelfth century CE, the time of the folding of the Roman Empire and of the slow rise of the medieval world of kings, counts, barons and of a vast mass of field serfs, appropriate conditions for reflection and for the elaboration of well-argued theology were few. In spite of this situation, the popular piety on Saint Joseph persevered and took roots whilst it was ignored in ecclesiastical circles. Carpenters specially held Saint Joseph as their patron and as such they prayed to him and held feasts in his honor.

In the thirteenth century CE there is an attempt of a more systematic reflection on Saint Joseph by the remarkable Franciscan thinker Pierre Jean Olivi (Peter John Olivi) (1248–1298 CE) who wrote a short treatise on Saint Joseph, the *Postilla super Matthaeum* (Lecture on Matthew).

3. See Maria, "Bibliografia fundamental Josefina"; this was reprinted in *Cahiers de Josephologie* (Montreal, 1966) and it provides a detailed historical account of research on Saint Joseph. Gauthier complied in a book with 1365 pages and more than 19700 titles on Saint Joseph, *Bibliographie sur Saint Joseph*. A good overview is presented by Gauthier and Bertrand in *Dictionnaire de Spiritualité*, "Joseph," 1301–21; See also Stramare, *Gesù lo chiamò Padre*; Stramare, "Giuseppe"; H. Rondet, " Saint Joseph"; Seitz, *Die Verehrung des hl. Joseph*; and concerning folklore, see *Enciclopedia Cattolica* 8:805ff.

The end of the thirteenth century and the whole of the fourteenth century is an important period for piety and theology rediscovering the holy humanity of Jesus. The spiritual experience of the mendicants, of Saint Francis of Assisi, of Saint Dominic, of the seven saints who founded the order of Servants of Mary was crucial for this happening. All of them wanted a return to the reading and preaching of the Gospel without the aid of interpretations and commentaries. And due to this we see a focus on Jesus' childhood, on the feasts of annunciation, on the birth of Christ, on nativity scenes, on the body and blood of Christ in the Eucharist, on the passion of Christ and on the Stations of the Cross. Everywhere we see people writing *Meditationes vitae Christi* (Meditations on the life of Christ). Within this scenario we see the appearance of references to the good Joseph and acts of devotion dedicated to him. Saint Margaret of Cortona (1247–97 CE) says daily two hundred "Our Father's" in honor of Saint Joseph.

The fifteenth and sixteenth centuries represent the apex of theological reflection on Saint Joseph and of efforts to spread worship for him. The first treatises focusing solely on Saint Joseph appeared. An emblematic figure of the time is the theologian and chancellor of the University of Paris, Jean de Charlier de Gerson (1363–1428) who corresponded with the Christian intelligentsia of the time. In his letters and sermons he provided a thorough and detailed reflection on Saint Joseph. Moreover, he wrote *Josephina*, a poem with 2957 verses in 12 books, which was written in outstanding Latin. The tone of the poem is of exalting Saint Joseph's virtues and gifts, such as that he had been sanctified from birth and freed by God of the lust of the flesh. Gerson puts Saint Joseph forward as the patron of families, nobles, manual workers, those who are dying, and the universal Church.

This period is also known as the age of the popular preachers who went around Europe, and who attracted to the squares thousands and thousands of people with their inflammatory sermons. Three of these popular preachers become known for divulging the cult of Saint Joseph. These are Saint Bernardino of Siena (1380–1444), Saint Vincent Ferrer (1350–1419) and Johann Eck (1486–1543).

Around the same time people started writing about the life of Saint Joseph, and these life accounts were very imaginative, and we also see the appearance of the first systematic treatises on Saint Joseph. The first of these treatises was written by the Dominican theologian Isidorus de

Isolano (ca 1475–1530), who published the *Summa de donis Sancti Joseph* (Sum of gifts of Saint Joseph). This text became a reference to all those who wrote treatises on Saint Joseph afterwards.

In 1535 Bernardin de Laredo combined piety with theology by writing his *Josephina*, where he presents Saint Joseph as a model for interior life. In doing so, he puts the piety of common people at the centre stage; that is, the piety of those who live Gospel values anonymously and on a daily basis without paying any notice to theological discussions and ecclesiastical guidance becomes central.

Two other authors helped greatly the spread of the cult of Saint Joseph: Andrés de Soto (ca 1553–1625) with his book *Libro de la vida y excellencias de el Bienaventurado San Joseph* (Book of the Life and Merits of the Blessed Saint Joseph), and Jérôme Gratien (1545–1614) who also wrote a *Josephina*, a long and detailed poem.

Francisco Suárez (1548–1617), the distinguished Jesuit theologian and professor at the University of Salamanca, had without doubt a great impact on all reflections on Saint Joseph that came after him, including my own argumentation in this book. In his *De mysterii vitae Christi* (The Mysteries of the Life of Christ), which forms the second volume of his larger work on the third part of the *Summa Theologica* of St. Thomas, he provides a great leap forward. Firstly, he places Saint Joseph in the hypostatic order. That is to say, Joseph is not merely a just man full of virtues and who is worthy of being the father of Jesus; Joseph is more than this, for he has such a deep relation with the mystery of incarnation that in a certain way he takes part in this mystery. Since God has a relation with Mary and Jesus, then the fact that Joseph is with them and has a mission towards them places Joseph in the same sphere of God also. I shall not argue this point any further here, for I shall refer to it later in this book in more detail since it is a central point to my argument.

Also extremely important for the cult of Saint Joseph is the figure of Saint Teresa of Avila (1515–82), who, in collaboration with Saint John of the Cross (1542–91), reformed the Carmelite order, was a prominent theologian, and was posthumously declared the first female Doctor of the Church. In her autobiography, *Life of Teresa of Avila*, she says she was cured at the age of twenty-six by the intercession of Saint Joseph. The first reformed Carmelite convent was put under the protection of Saint Joseph on the August 24, 1562, and for this reason it is named Saint Joseph of Avila. The other eleven reformed Carmelite convents are also put under the protection of Saint Joseph. In her autobiography she states: "I do not to this day ever having asked him [Saint Joseph] for anything that he did not grant me."[4] And to those who find it difficult to pray she advises: "If anyone cannot find a master to teach him prayer, he should take this glorious saint for master, and he will not go astray on the road."[5]

The influence that Saint Teresa had on Spain, which was the imperial superpower of the time, and which dominated a great part of the known world, helped tremendously the cult of Saint Joseph and theological reflection upon him. Around the same time, we also see the appearance of the first litanies on Saint Joseph.

The seventeenth and eighteenth century are considered to be the golden age of reflection and devotion towards Saint Joseph. Writings and treatises on Saint Joseph appear in great numbers around the whole of Europe, especially in France and Spain, which were the dominating powers of the time.

Cardinal Pierre de Bérulle (1575–1629) and his circle declared themselves to be devotees of Saint Joseph. In his well-known *Discours de l'Etat et des Grandeurs de Jésus* (Discourse on the State and Grandeur of Jesus) of 1623 he says: "Joseph is the chief-place of God in the noblest part of his State and Empire."[6]

Jean-Jacques Olier (1608–57) founder of the seminary of Lazarist priests of Saint Suplice, who grew in number in the ranks of the Church, put this new initiative under the patronage of Saint Joseph. In his book *La vie intérier de la Très Saint Vierge* (The Interior Life of the Most Holy Virgin) he presents Joseph as "the image of the purity of the eternal Father," and "in him the Father markedly expresses all of its divine perfections, its wisdom, prudence, love and mercy."

The two famous panegyrics of Jacques-Bénigne Bossuet (1627–1704) were written around this time: the *Depositum Custodi* of 1656 and 1659, and the *Quaesivit sibi Deus*, of 1657 and 1670. These are considered to be the most beautiful pious writings about Saint Joseph, at least insofar as the French language is concerned.

For my argument in this book it is important to mention Louis-François d'Argentan (1615–80), who wrote *Conférences theologique*

4. Teresa of Avila, *The Life of Saint Theresa of Avila*, 47.

5. Ibid., 48.

6. De Bérulle, *Oeuvres Completes*, 3.1.

et spirituelles sur les Grandeurs de la tres-Vierge Marie, Mere de Dieu (Theological and Spiritual Discussions on the Grandeurs of the Virgin Mary, Mother of God) of 1680, and where he states that Joseph is "the shadow of the celestial Father." As I shall argue later, this expression "shadow of the Father" opens up the possibility of understanding Saint Joseph as the personification of the Father.

Another great thinker of the time is Saint Francis de Sales (1567–1622), whose influence, especially on Saint Joana de Chantal (1572–1641), his close friend and confidant, spread throughout the whole of France and Europe. In his *19ème Entretien* he deals with Saint Joseph in a very refined theological fashion, and does so with great devotion.

During this period and because of the advent of the Enlightenment and individuality, we see the rise of a kind of piety that conforms with the requirements of the time. The interior life and the personal path leading to Christ and to the Church are ideas that are cultivated at the time, especially among the Jesuits. It is within this context that Saint Joseph is rediscovered as the master of interior life lived within the family and in the silence of work and of daily tasks. Around this time there is also the rise of many secular movements, Marian congregations and various secular associations connected to new religious congregations or around the various Jesuit colleges. One of these movements, the Assembly of Friends, became famous for its devotion to Saint Joseph. This movement was formed by laymen and professionals who, despite being in the middle of society, cultivated the interior life. The Assembly of Friends reached various parts of Europe and it has the holy family as its model, for in the holy family there is a deep union of the human and the divine, which is something that the members of the Assembly of Friends wished to emulate. Joseph was seen as the head of the family, first as a husband and then as a father.[7]

In Spain the publication of books and treatises on Saint Joseph continued during this period, and it is worth noting here the book *In caput primum Matthaei* (On the First Chapter of Matthew) by Pedro Morales which was published in 1614. In this book Morales transcribes through long citations everything important that previously had been written about Saint Joseph. The Spanish missionaries took the cult of Saint Joseph to the entire Latin America and to the Far East. In the year 1555 Mexico

---

7. See the study on this issue by Poutet, "Saint Joseph dans la spiritualité."

was put under the patronage of Saint Joseph, and this is something that the French missionaries only did to Canada in the year 1624. Everywhere we see novenas, small divine offices, *Ave Joseph*, and crown rosaries of Saint Joseph, and Wednesday is dedicated to Saint Joseph.

During the seventeenth century we also see the appearance of the first congregations dedicated to Saint Joseph. And this is a sign of the spread of the cult of Saint Joseph and of a continuous tradition of reflections on the figure of Saint Joseph. The very first congregation was established in 1517 in Genova, the Daughters of Saint Joseph, who were influenced by Saint Catherine of Siena (1347–80). Then, in 1620 we see the appearance in Rome of the Josephites; in 1638 in Bordeaux, France, the Daughters of Saint Joseph; in 1643 in La Flèche, France, the Hospitallers of Saint Joseph; in 1648 in Le Puy, France, the Sisters of Saint Joseph; in 1660 in Lyon, France, the Missionaries of Saint Joseph; and finally, in 1694 in Montreal, Canada, the Hospitallers of Saint Joseph of the Cross. And a number of other congregations continue to appear afterwards.

Between 1517 and 1980 172 religious communities which had Saint Joseph as their patron saint were founded, being 51 male communities and 121 female communities. Just in the United States, 36 communities dedicated to Saint Joseph were established. Many parishes in Brazil have fraternities of Saint Joseph, which visit the sick in hospitals and provide support to those who are terminally ill.

All language about Saint Joseph during these past centuries was characterized by the maximization, exaltation, and by an exacerbated glorification of the virtues and gifts of the saint, and this is something that has little to do with the historic figure of Joseph, working away in his workshop, living alongside his family, experiencing the spirituality of the poor of Yahweh, the "good people."

The eighteenth century is characterized by a general decline of the Church, which was undermined by the Enlightenment's rationalism and scientific approach. The Church and its theology are considered to be things of the dark ages, and such a view, which circulated at the time, impinged negatively on the Christian intelligentsia, which felt cornered and the need to provide justifications about itself. Within such a scenario it is understandable that research and creativity did not encounter favorable ground, especially in connection to Saint Joseph.

However, missionaries and popular preachers, such as Saint Leonard of Port Maurice (1676–1751), who set Italy ablaze with the power of his preaching, did not let the flame of devotion to Saint Joseph be extinguished. Saint Alphonsus Liguori (1696–1787) founded the order of Redemptorists, which was put under the patronage of Saint Joseph, and wrote a book of novenas to Saint Joseph. Saint Joseph is especially referred to as the Patron Saint of the Dying and the Saint of the Good Death. Insofar as theologians are concerned, it is worth mentioning here Antonio Peralta (1668–1736) from Mexico who published an extensive treatise in 1727, *Dissertationes scholasticae de Sancto Joseph* (Scholastic Dissertations on Saint Joseph). In Brazil we see the spread of the Devotion to the Three Hearts of Jesus, Mary, and Joseph, which arrived from Portugal and which named the city of Três Corações (Three Hearts) in the Brazilian state of Minas Gerais.

In the nineteenth century, when the anti-clerical storm abated despite the ongoing process of secularization, the devotional interest on Saint Joseph resumed. Saint Joseph had a guaranteed presence in the great manuals used to teach theology in the colleges and seminaries, such as the manuals by M. J. Scheeben, L. Billot, F. Egger, and J. Kleutgen, to cite a few.[8]

It is interesting to mention three authors here who corroborate my views: G. M. Piccirelli, a Jesuit who published in 1890 and 1891 a series of papers in the *Bolletino della Lega Sacerditale* (Napoli-Sorrento) which are entitled "Della preminenza assoluta di San Giuseppe nell'ordine estrinseco dell'unione ipostatica" (On the absolute pre-eminence of Saint Joseph in the extrinsic order of the hypostatic union); L. Bellovet and his article *La Science Catholique* in 1894 which is entitled "Le Père de la misericorde, Saint Joseph appartient-il à l'ordre hypostatique?" (The Father of mercy, Saint Joseph, does he belong to the hypostatic order?); and lastly, the orator F. W. Faber, who presents Saint Joseph in his works on spirituality, which were greatly circulated within the Church especially between the years 1853 and 1860, as "the shadow of the figure of the eternal Father."

In the twentieth century we see the studies on Saint Joseph maturing a great deal through thorough exegetical investigations, through a perusal of all the texts from the Fathers of the Church and from the main theologians in the tradition, through research on popular devotion to

8. See Gauthier, "Saint Joseph d'aprés les Théologiens de la Fin du XIX Siècle"; see also Stöhr, "Zur Theologie und Verehrung des heiligen Joseph in Deutschland seit der Säkularisation."

Saint Joseph, and through the appearance of real treatises on Josephology. It is worth noting here, for their seriousness and rigor, the studies by T. Stramare, R. Gauthier, G. M. Bertrand, A. Doze, B. Llamera, P. Grelot, among others.

The creation of a series of centers of study on Josephology was of extreme importance, centers with their respective journals and library collections. They maintain a continuous scholarship, foster research, and offer a systematic understanding about Saint Joseph and about his place in the intentions of the Mystery.

Also worthy of mention is the journal *Estudios Josefinos*, which was founded in 1947 by the Barefoot Carmelites of Valladolid, and the research center that was founded in 1957.

The priests of Holy Cross congregation founded in 1953 in the Saint Joseph's Oratory of Mount-Royal, Montreal, Canada, which is the biggest in the world, the prestigious journal *Cahiers de Joséphologie*. Since 1952 the Oratory houses a research center with one of the best library collections on Saint Joseph, and I personally have benefited from visiting it. Other research centers were created in Viterbo (1952) and in Milan (1963) in Italy, in Mexico (1963), in Kalisz (1969) in Poland, and in Louvain (1978) in Belgium.

The First International Symposium on Saint Joseph occurred from November 29 to December 6, 1970, in Rome, and provided a new impetus to research, and allowed the main researchers in the area to meet. These academic meetings continue regularly and the records are published by the above mentioned centers of Valladolid, Montreal, and Mexico.

Today the field of Josephology is well established. Certainly, there is still a lot to be systematically researched in the field. However, we do not need to refer to the theology about Saint Joseph in inverted commas, as Cardinal Dubois did in his book as late as 1927, as if the reflections on Saint Joseph were not worthy of the field of theology.[9]

And insofar as my central thesis in this book, the issue of Joseph being the personification of the Father and part of the hypostatic order, three names are fundamental: Father Paul-Eugène Charbonneau, who lived for many years and died in Brazil, and his doctoral thesis *Saint Joseph appartient-il à l'ordre de l'union hypostatique?* (Does Saint Joseph Belong to the Hypostatic Order?) of 1961; A. Doze, *Joseph, ombre du Père*

9. Cardinal Dubois, "Théologie de Saint Joseph," in *Saint Joseph*, 133–45.

(Joseph, Shadow of the Father) of 1989; and the writings of friar Adauto Schumaker, a Brazilian who lived in the Amazon region, and who first explicitly spoke about Joseph as "the personification of the Father."[10]

I shall refer to their views and try to expand their views so as to maintain without a doubt that Saint Joseph appears in the history of salvation as the personification of the Father, just as Mary is the personification of the Holy Spirit and Jesus of the Word.

SAINT JOSEPH IN LITURGY AND IN PAPAL WRITINGS

We do not know exactly when the Church's veneration of Saint Joseph started. Naturally, he was connected with the religions feasts in honor of Mary (Annunciation and Dormition) and in the honor of Christ (Christmas and Presentation to the Temple). Saint Joseph's name was always received with respect and care for he was the husband of Mary and father to Jesus.

It is only in the eighth and ninth centuries that the first narratives of worship to Saint Joseph appeared in the Coptic Church. He was remembered as Joseph, the carpenter, on August 2. Around the same time in the Byzantine church Saint Joseph is celebrated on movable dates around Christmas time, but always along with the magi kings. And in the eighth century we see the appearance in the Roman Church of liturgical worship of Saint Joseph, husband of Mary, or as the nurturing father of Jesus in the other regional churches—the chosen date here is always August 19.

In the thirteenth century the Benedictines of the Saint Lawrence Abbaye in Liège, Belgium, had already compiled a divine office and attached it to the mass in honor of Saint Joseph, and this is evidence that the worship of Saint Joseph was already organized and implemented.

It is to the great merit of the priests of the order of the Servants of Mary, who, in 1334, inserted in their general chapter their decision to celebrate Saint Joseph on March 19, and they were followed by the Franciscans in 1399. These two mendicant orders were and continue to be directly connected to the pope and are allowed to take their liturgy and own religious feasts everywhere in the universal Church. As they were orders that were very popular, they ended up greatly spreading the devotion to Saint Joseph amongst the people, but they also spread

10. Schumaker, "A Trindade mediadora," n.p.

the devotion to Saint Joseph in an official fashion through their liturgy. However, it was only later that the popes created the official religious feasts of Saint Joseph.

Pope Sixtus IV (1471–84) was the first to welcome the Feast of Saint Joseph as a simple feast in the Breviary and in the Missal. Gregory XV (1621) established the Feast of Saint Joseph as a principal feast on March 19 following calls from the kings of Austria and Spain. During the pontificate of Pius IX, which was one of the longest in history (1846–78), a number of petitions directed to the Congregation of Rites asking that Saint Joseph be proclaimed the Patron of the Church arrived from all corners of Christendom; this is a time when the Pontifical States are being attacked and in which the process of secularization in Germany and Austria threatened convents and dioceses with property confiscation by the state. At the end of the First Vatican Council, which was interrupted by the Franco-Prussian War (1870), the pope officially declared Saint Joseph as the Patron Saint of the Universal Church on December 8, 1870, via a decree of the Sacred Congregation of Rites (*Quaemadmodum Deus*); furthermore, his important feast must be celebrated on March 19.

This is a curious set up which reflects the grandiloquent style of the time, and which is in contrast to the situation of the poor historic Joseph of Nazareth. The *Acta Apostolicae Sedis 6* (1870) says: "Just as with Joseph of Egypt, God established Joseph of Nazareth as master and prince of his house and of his property; and the most precious treasures were put under his stewardship."

Leo XIII (1878–1903) published on August 15, 1889, the first encyclical on Saint Joseph, the *Quamquam pluries*. Theologically this is a weak work but it has encouraged devotion to the saint by dedicating the whole month of March to Saint Joseph, the month of Saint Joseph, and every Wednesday, and especially March 19, as the great religious feast dedicated to the Patron Saint of the Universal Church. His social encyclical, *Rerum Novarum*, follows a line that disregards social classes and inevitable conflicts and presents Saint Joseph as the patron saint that serves all independent of social status, as the patron saint of couples, of family fathers, of those consecrated to virginity, of the bankrupt nobles, of the successful rich so that they be generous, of the poor, of the needy, and of the workers because their condition requires special protection by Saint Joseph so that they can understand that their humble profession does not need to be insignificant, and through virtues can be ennobled.

Pius XI (1922–39) introduced a curiosity: in the feast of Saint Joseph of March 19, 1930, he declared Saint Joseph as the patron saint of Russia, and in an encyclical, the *Divini Redemptoris*, which was published on the day of the feast of Saint Joseph in 1937, he asks intercessions of Saint Joseph against communism. In a speech on May 19, 1935, to the clergy in Rome he suggests that Saint Joseph belongs to the hypostatic order, or at least that he received a revelation regarding this.

Pius XII (1939–58) proclaimed May 1 as the Day of Saint Joseph, the Worker.

John XXIII (1958–63) entrusted the Second Vatican Council to Saint Joseph and introduced the name of Saint Joseph in the cannon of the mass: "Saint Joseph, Husband of Mary."

John Paul II (1978–2005) showed great devotion to Saint Joseph, who is always cited in his various encyclicals. His Apostolic Exortation *Redemptoris Custos* of August 15, 1989, was dedicated to Saint Joseph, and he writes about the figure of Saint Joseph and of Saint Joseph's mission in the life of Christ and of the Church; this encyclical was written to celebrate the centenary of the encyclical of Leo XIII, the *Quamquam pluries*, the only one that had been written on Saint Joseph. In this document the pope takes up again data in the tradition. He fundamentally follows the outline of the Gospels and presents all events in which Saint Joseph appears. He does not follow the modern exegesis, which has contributed with so many elements to the tradition, he rather prefers to guide himself by the interpretation that was put forward by the Fathers of Church, which is more of a spiritual and pastoral nature. Noteworthy here is part V, "The Primacy of the Interior Life", where he makes concrete suggestions to the life of the faithful. At a certain point in the document, however, he advances in the direction of my thesis in this book when he asserts that Saint Joseph's human fatherhood was "taken up" in the mystery of incarnation and in this way it gained an hypostatic dimension.[11]

On May 25, 1982, John Paul II canonized one of the most important persons in the spreading of the cult to Saint Joseph, namely, André Bessete (1845–1937), a religious layman and semi-literate of the congregation of the Holy Cross Brothers, Montreal, Canada, and who was the porter during his entire life in the Collège Notre Dame. When he was very young he was very sick and he made a promise to Saint Joseph. If

---

11. John Paul II, *Redemporis Custos*, n. 21.

he was accepted as a religious man he would make all efforts to build a church dedicated to Saint Joseph. He was a man of many virtues and extreme humbleness, who attracted crowds and who consoled and cured many with his prayers. He succeeded in building Saint Joseph's Oratory, in Mount-Royal, Montreal, Canada, which is the biggest sanctuary dedicated to Saint Joseph in the world.

In conclusion, I have established that the figure of Saint Joseph slowly gained space in the Christian consciousness until it fully blossomed within the Church. Everyone had a hand in this, especially the popular strata which are connected to the Mystery more through experience than through reflection. According to the well-known Josephologist Roland Gauthier, the Holy See was the last to embrace the devotion to Saint Joseph.[12] The Holy See was not particularly forthcoming with the spreading of the cult of Saint Joseph and with the introduction of Saint Joseph's name in the cannon of the mass. It is therefore symptomatic of this situation that Saint Joseph was proclaimed Patron Saint of the Universal Church through a decree of the Sacred Congregation of Rites on December 8, 1870, and not directly by Pope Pius IX.

However much the centers and journals on Saint Joseph have spread, theology has failed to sufficiently incorporate the figure and the meaning of Saint Joseph in its treatises.[13] There is still a predominant lack of originality and organization between the truths within the unique truth: the self-communication of God-Trinity to his creation. If this perspective becomes central then it will be easier for Christians to understand that not only the Son personified itself in Jesus, but also that the Holy Spirit personified itself in Mary, and the Father in Joseph.

Joseph who came from obscurity and who first saw the light, Joseph who remained always in silence to better express the Mystery without a name, continues to invite the Church and theology to develop a unified understanding. This understanding is able to display the unconditional love and infinite affection of God-Trinity for the human family, and concretely, for Jesus, Mary, and Joseph. Jesus, Mary, and Joseph anticipate that which is the destiny of all: the complete immersion in the Trinitarian life and communion.

---

12. See Gauthier, "La Proclamation de Saint Joseph," 29–50.

13. See De la Noi, *De La Redemptoris Custos a la Teología Dogmática*, 171–75.

7

Saint Joseph of God: The Order of Hypostatic Union

I have now reached an important point in my reflections on this issue. Joseph can only be properly understood within the inter-play of relations that his person and his function establish. There is a trinity in Nazareth, which is constituted by the family Jesus-Mary-Joseph. The Holy Spirit entered this family by overshadowing Mary (cf. Luke 1:35) and the eternal Son also entered this family by overshadowing Jesus (cf. John 1:14). These facts impinge on Joseph, for Mary is his wife and Jesus is his son. The question here is then: How does Joseph relate with the divine persons, which are present in his family? The answer to this question is connected to the concept *hypostatic order*.

WHAT IS THE HYPOSTATIC ORDER?

The word hypostatic comes from *hypostasis*, which in classical and ecclesiastical Greek stands for "person." As I have stated above, the Person of the Holy Spirit and the Person of the Son respectively overshadowed Mary and Jesus. This extraordinary event establishes the hypostatic order, that is to say, establishes a dimension and a way of being and of acting that is proper to these divine Persons. Although the hypostatic order is particular to the divine Persons, it is open to participation because the divine Persons graciously "took up" Mary and Jesus into their divine reality.

Does Saint Joseph fit in the hypostatic order? Why should we leave him out? There are excellent reasons for placing Saint Joseph alongside his wife and his son. What we know for certain is the following: he has an immediate and close relation, and he maintains this relation, with Mary, in whom the Holy Spirit is, and with Jesus, in whom the Son is. This relation allows us to say that, at least indirectly, Saint Joseph belongs to the hypostatic order, for we cannot really think of Mary and Jesus without Saint Joseph as a husband or as a father. Let me now demonstrate in more detail the relations at play here.

Firstly, Saint Joseph has a proper relation with Mary. He was connected to Mary even before her virginal conception; he was connected to Mary by a marital link, be this through their engagement, which for the understanding of the time had the same status as a marriage, or through the wedding ceremony that took place soon after the annunciation of Mary's pregnancy by the Holy Spirit. He is Mary's husband. Mary is his wife. And in a certain way Saint Joseph has, through Mary, a relation with the Holy Spirit.

And because Joseph is a real and true husband he also establishes a second singular relation with Jesus by becoming a matrimonial father that cares, accompanies, protects, and educates Jesus. This son of his that he cares for is the Son of God. Saint Joseph has, therefore, a singular relation with the second Person of the Trinity. Thus, here there is another proper hypostatic relation.

In the *Redemptoris Custos* of John Paul II it is explicitly stated: "Together with human nature, all that is human, and especially the family—as the first dimension of man's existence in the world—is also taken up in Christ. Within this context, Joseph's human fatherhood was also 'taken up' in the mystery of Christ's Incarnation."[1]

My reasoning is logical and consistent with doctrine. I am amazed by the fact that this kind of reasoning was not perceived by theologians for fifteen centuries. There was, however, a process that progressed towards this knowledge, a process whose stages can be reconstructed as is currently being done by prominent Josephologists.[2] I have identified five main stages to this process and I shall deal with these below.

1. John Paul II, *Redemptoris Custos,* n. 21.

2. See the book *Saint Joseph appartient-il à l'ordre de l'union hypostatique?*; this volume includes a number of articles with the same title which appeared in the *Cahiers de Joséphologie* 7 (1959) 5–33; 195–221; *Cahiers de Joséphologie* 8 (1960) 41–74; 293–318; and it also encompasses the article "L'Appartenance de Saint Joseph à l'Ordre de l'Union Hypostatique et son Rôle de Patron de l'Eglise Universelle," *Cahiers de Joséphologie* 2 (1955) 241–74. See also the following bibliography: Solá i Carrio, "Pertenencia de San José al Orden Hipostático"; Schreder, " S. Joseph et l'Union Hypostatique"; Samson, "San Giuseppe e l'Ordine dell'Unione Ipostatica"; de la Immaculada, OCA, "Pertenencia de San José al Orden de la Unión Hipostático"; Pujiula, "Aptitud de San José para el Orden

SAINT JOSEPH TAKES PART IN THE ECONOMY
OF SALVATION

In the first stage there is talk of Saint Joseph's collaboration in the economy of salvation, and more specifically in the mystery of incarnation. "Economy of salvation" is a theological and liturgical technical expression, which was also taken up by the Church's official language, that stands for the historical process, and its various phases, through which God progressively enters into human life and history, fulfills his covenant, and offers his grace and salvation. Saint Joseph occupies a very important place in this process, for through him Jesus enters into the human family as a common person.

The first to explicitly insert Saint Joseph in the economy of salvation was Saint John Chrysostom (347–407); then Saint Augustine (354–430) with more reflection; and then, in a very clear and elegant way the chancellor of the University of Paris, Jean Charlier de Gerson (1363–1428).[3] This led to the culmination of this stage when Isidorus de Isolano (ca. 1475–1530) published the *Summa de donis Sancti Joseph* (All the Gifts of Saint Joseph) in 1522, which is the first treatise on Saint Joseph and which clearly states the relation between Saint Joseph and the divine plan of salvation.

Isolano argues that Joseph is the closest person to Jesus, the incarnate Word, because Joseph is the husband of Mary who became pregnant by the Holy Spirit, and because he accepted Mary's virginal motherhood as well as the paternity of Jesus. Isolano emphasizes a number of times in his various works: "Joseph was a just consonant with the Holy Spirit's testimony; for this reason and more than anyone else, Joseph was or-

---

Hipostático"; Palmier, "Pertenencia de San José al Orden de la Unión Hipostática"; A. Michel, "Appartenance de S. Joseph à l'Ordre de l'Union Hypostatique"; McGinnis, "The Holiness of Saint Joseph and the Order of Hypostatic Union"; Llamera, "Pertenece San José al Orden Hipostático?"; Llamera, "La Relación de San José con el Orden Hipostático"; Llamera, *Teologia de San José*, 115–43; Iglesias, "La Paternidad de San José le Relaciona con el Orden Hipostático"; Sauvé, *Le Mystère de Joseph*, esp. 116–30; Gauthier, *La Paternité de Saint Joseph*, 150–51.

3. I would like to call the reader's attention to the beautiful comment by Jean de Charlier de Gerson in a sermon to the priests taking part in the Council of Constance (1414–18): "I wish the words to explain this most high mystery that has been hidden for centuries would come in abundantly, that is to say, the mystery of this admirable and venerable Trinity that is Jesus, Mary and Joseph"; *Sermo de Nativitate gloriosae Virginis Mariae*, in *Concilio Constantiensi*, Tertia Pars Operum: Paris, 1606, t. II, cons. 4, col. 140, cited by PE. Charbonneau, *Saint Joseph*, 82–83.

dained very close and immediately to Christ . . . He was ordained with the education and with the paternity of Christ. As a consequence of this Joseph, after Mary, is that which is most directly ordained to Christ."[4]

The idea of Saint Joseph's hypostatic ordination is implicit in Isolano's works but it was not formulated in technical terms.

SAINT JOSEPH BELONGS TO THE HYPOSTATIC ORDER

The technical formulation was put forward by Francisco Suárez (1548–1617), the great Spanish Jesuit theologian of the sixteenth century, and this inaugurates the second phase. Let me quote a passage from Suárez, which is very important for my thesis in this book. Suárez draws a parallel between the mission and the mystery of the apostles and the mission and the mystery of Joseph. I quote:

> I understand that the mystery of the apostles is the most excellent of all the mysteries instituted by Jesus Christ in his Church. However, I believe that it is possible to legitimately affirm that there is a probability that the mystery or the mission of Saint Joseph is even more perfect because, in reality, he belongs to a higher order. In fact, there are mysteries that only belong to the order of grace, and within this order the apostles occupy the highest position. And without a doubt, and because of this highest position, the apostles must have been given more graces and more charisms. There are other mysteries that are connected to the order of hypostatic union. This order is by nature more perfect than the order of grace. I understand that the mystery of Saint Joseph is found within the order of hypostatic union, however, at a lower level. And therefore, this mystery is over and above all other mysteries that belong to the order of grace because it belongs to a higher order . . . The mystery of Saint Joseph does not belong to the New Testament and neither does it, to be truthful, to the Old Testament, it rather belongs to the author of both, to their cornerstone, to Jesus Christ, who unites both testaments.[5]

For the first time, a remarkable Catholic theologian dared to think about the figure of Saint Joseph within the context of the hypostatic union of the Word, and moreover, as a reality that belongs to this order: "I understand that the mystery of Saint Joseph is found within the order of

4. Isolani, *Summa de donis Sancti Joseph.*

5. Suárez, "Comentarium."

hypostatic union." Pay attention, however, that Suàrez does not say that the person of Saint Joseph, but Saint Joseph's mystery, which is the same as saying his function, belongs to the hypostatic order. Later in this book I shall try to go further than this and argue that the person of Saint Joseph belongs to the hypostatic order, however, in connection with the Person of the celestial Father.

Taking Suàrez as their starting point, various theologians have engaged in research on the nature of the order and whether it is implicit or explicit and if it is immediate or mediate.

After Suàrez it is worth mentioning the Franciscan Josephologist Juan de Carthagena who developed his ideas around the year 1613. He takes up Suàrez's thesis and explains it in a precise and imperative way. He writes:

> Mary and Joseph were elevated to the service of the incarnated Word: Mary to provide him with the substance of his flesh and Joseph to provide sustenance . . . As a consequence of this, after Mary, Saint Joseph was the most immediately ordained to the humanity of Christ . . . this is the lowest grade of the hypostatic order, but it is so excellent that it is over and above all other orders . . . of angels, of seraphim, of cherubim, of apostles. This later, the order of apostles, is ordained to the mystical body of the Church whilst the mystery of Saint Joseph is ordained to the natural body of Christ.

After de Carthagena's argumentation various theologians tackled this question on basically the same terms. The formulation *pertinet ad unionem hypostaticam*, that is, "belongs to the hypostatic union," is repeated again and again. The culmination of this stage is found in a text of the Provincial Council of Poitiers (1868), which echoes the thesis defended by Suàrez and his followers. It states: "Christian piety does not stray far when it attributes to Saint Joseph such a great glory and immense power and concord with that which the learned Suàrez observed about Saint Joseph's connection with the most distinguished order of hypostatic union."

SAINT JOSEPH BELONGS TO THE HYPOSTATIC ORDER: AN UNDISPUTED IDEA

The third phase is the phase in which the idea that Saint Joseph belongs to the hypostatic order, an idea which was first thought by Suàrez and then elaborated by de Carthagena, was disseminated. It is no longer about justifying the idea; rather, the idea is by now considered accepted and known amongst theologians. The important thing by now is to increasingly disseminate this idea.

As Charbonneau says:

> In order to negate the fact (that Saint Joseph) belongs to the hypostatic order, the concrete circumstances through which God willed the incarnation would have to be unknown to us. By taking into account these circumstances, which cannot be ignored, we can see that Joseph is connected to Mary because the Word dwelt amongst men, and this is Joseph's and Mary's unique and exclusive purpose, this is their irrefutable purpose because it is written in revelation; and this purpose places both of them, each on its own right, in the order of hypostatic union.

In other words, there is no real and truthful incarnation without the connection with Mary and Joseph. And this connection implies that Saint Joseph belongs to the hypostatic order.

It was then a question of researching the implications and searching for an adequate way of expressing how Saint Joseph belongs to the hypostatic order. Discussions have said that Joseph occupies the lowest place in the order of hypostatic union. This is of no importance. What is important here is Joseph's relation with the two divine Persons, the Word and the Holy Spirit.

Theologians speculate: Is Saint Joseph within the hypostatic order? Does he serve the hypostatic order? Does he participate in the hypostatic order? Does he belong in the hypostatic order? Is Saint Joseph's relation to the hypostatic order immediate or mediate? Is Saint Joseph's relation to the hypostatic order intrinsically physical or intrinsically ethical? The answers to all these questions, as it often happens in theology, encompass a number of subtleties, distinctions, and sub-distinctions, which end up being more confusing than clarifying to the issue.[6] The methodology

---

6. For a detailed discussion on this issue, which is always carried out within the Aristotelian-Thomist perspective of mediaeval philosophy and theology, see Charbonneau, *Saint Joseph*, 113–36; another detailed discussion, which is conducted within the same perspective is found in other authors, such as Llamera, *Pertenece Saint José*, 251–82; and it is worth referring here to 269: "Saint Joseph cooperates in the 'constitution' of the hypostatic order in a truthful, singular, extrinsic, moral and mediate way."

used is almost exclusively derived from medieval metaphysics, which is static and formal.

I do not want to disqualify this kind of theological methodology, but I have decided to follow a different methodology, which is linked to a proper phenomenological understanding and to the sense of totality that is present in divine and human events.

I would say the following: to be a father constitutes a complex phenomenon that starts with the biological generation, then it involves physical nourishing, human, psychological, and moral guidance in the process of individualization, until it reaches the inter-relation of mutual recognition. When Joseph took Mary as his wife, when he accepted (not without being reluctant) her pregnancy, when he took her to his house and welcomed the child that was born, Joseph fulfilled *ex officio* all the functions of husband and father in a truly affirmative way. Nevertheless, it is important to recognize that Joseph is not a father in a strictly genetic-biological sense, for Jesus was not originated from him according to the unanimous testimonies of the early church. Even so it is still fair to say that in an anthropological and sociological way Joseph is the real father because the paternal mission and functions (i.e., his mystery, as the theologians holding the thesis that he belongs to the hypostatic order would say) were completely taken on by him in the various stages of constitution, of growth, and of maturing in the life of Jesus.

It is not possible to think about the incarnation of the Word in Jesus without the presence of Joseph. He belongs to the event of incarnation, be this as Mary's husband or as Jesus' father. His belonging to the hypostatic order is not metaphorical, and it is not for morality's sake either; it is rather real, concrete and truthful. Certainly, Joseph would never formulate the events that took place with him in this fashion. It would be strange and even incomprehensible for him to hear that he "belongs to the hypostatic order." This is my discourse, it is not Joseph's. My discourse is cultural and theological. Joseph's discourse was also cultural and theological but it was expressed within the categories of his spiritual tradition, which is biblical.

The sense of Joseph's discourse is the following: he feels involved in an event that mysteriously has to do with God. He embraces, with surprise and anguish, his involvement (cf. Matt 1:19), perhaps without understanding its full implications. But as he is a man that leads his life in the light of God (as any other just man in Israel (cf. Matt 1:19) and because he has a lot of faith in the intent of the Mystery, he kept all these things in his heart, just as did Mary (cf. Luke 2:51).

This completely un-ambitious and upright attitude of entrusting the Unknown-known is enough to confirm his active participation and his substantial cooperation in the mystery of the Spirit overshadowing Mary and of the Word dwelling in Jesus. Joseph is thus connected with God's self-communication to the world, in the form of personalization in Mary and of incarnation in Jesus.

However, it is important to emphasize here that the theological literature rarely tackled the relation of Joseph with the Holy Spirit through Mary. And it is only recently that theologians (but not the theologians of the ecclesiastical magisterium) started to consider the relation of Joseph, terrestrial father of Jesus, to the celestial Father. He is presented as the shadow of the Father in the fourth stage of the reflection on Saint Joseph.[7]

SAINT JOSEPH: THE "SHADOW" OF THE FATHER

Let me explain this kind of understanding in more detail. Firstly, it is important to bear in mind that Jesus is son of Joseph, which is something that is clearly said in the New Testament (cf. Matt 13:54–56; Luke 4:22; John 1:45; 6:42). And there emerges an undeniable connection between the humble father of Nazareth and the celestial Father in virtue of the paternity of both. What is the nature of this connection?

François-Louis d'Argentan, in his well-known *Conférences Theologique et Spirituelles sur les Grandeurs de la tres-Vierge Marie, Mere de Dieu* (Theological and Spiritual Discussions on the Grandeurs of the Virgin Mary, Mother of God) of 1680, tried to explain the nature of this connection first. He clearly states that Saint Joseph is the "shadow of the Father." He writes:

> Oh invaluable glory of the great Saint Joseph! He is the shadow of
> the Father. He represents the person of the Father to his unique

---

7. See the important work of A. Doze, *Joseph, ombre du Père*, especially chapt. 5: "L'Ombre du Père," 83–103; see also Ephraïm, *Joseph, un Père*, 124–33; Sauvé, *Le Mystère de Joseph*, especially 119–22; Their approach does not follow my line of reasoning here, that is, of a true hypostatic relation of the person of the Father with the person of Joseph. These authors follow a line of reasoning that establishes the hypostatic relation through the virtues, qualities, and affinities of the celestial Father being reflected in the terrestrial father.

> Son. He even wishes that he be given the honour of being called a
> father in the place of the celestial Father. I openly call Saint Joseph
> the father of the incarnate Word, as it is written in the gospels, for
> he is the shadow of the Father and the shadow is no other thing
> than the body itself of which it is a shadow.

This is a very audacious statement. Joseph is not only the shadow of the
Father, that is, the mysterious presence of the Father, but also the embodiment of the Father, of which he is the shadow. This is at the heart
of the thesis I will defend in more detail later in this book: Joseph is the
personification of the Father. But let me dwell a little longer on the expression *shadow of the Father.*

This expression is derived from the biblical expression "shadow of
the Spirit," or for those, like me, who follow the Greek text this is usually
translated as "the Spirit will put his tent over" Mary (cf. Luke 1:35). In order to understand the meaning of the expression "shadow of the father," I
need to explain four concepts: to dwell, tent, cloud, and shadow.

In Hebrew there is not an exact word for "to dwell." Because the Jews
were either nomads, semi-nomads, or very often, exiled, they did not
have the experience of dwelling as something properly permanent. They
lived wandering between places. To dwell safely and permanently was
one of the things the Jewish people most longed for (cf. Deut 12:8–10;
Amos 9:15; Isa 33:20). But they never achieved this fully and for this
reason they reiterate: only God has a permanent dwelling in heaven and
his holy temple on earth in Jerusalem (cf. Deut 12:5–14; 1 Kgs 8:11); we
are only pilgrims.

To express "to dwell" they used the expression "put the tent up,"
which is characteristic of nomads and wandering peoples. "To put the
tent up" is *shakan* in Hebrew (from which the word *shekinah*, the presence of God radiating from his tent, is derived) and the Seventy (the first
translators, those who translated the Hebrew Bible into Greek in northern
Egypt in the first century BCE) translated *shakan* as *skiasein* or *episkiasen*
which means "to open and put up the tent" or simply "to dwell." Note that
the Greek verb *skiasein* is related to the word *skene* which means "tent."

The clouds formed the tent of Yahweh (cf. Ps 97:2; 2 Sam 22:12).
Why clouds? Because they cast a shadow, and the shadow—this is the
theology of the first 40 chapters of Exodus (cf. Exod 40:36–38)—symbolizes the maternal and protective presence of God, a presence that reveals
itself by hiding and that is hidden by revealing itself. The cloud accompa-

nies the Jewish people in their wanderings around the desert. When the cloud moved, they wandered. When the cloud did not move, then they remained where they were. In fact, the cloud is a symbol for the mysterious character of the presence of God, something that we see but that we cannot touch and which is something that is luminous and dark, something that appears and vanishes, something that fascinates and strikes fear at the same time (cf. Exod 14:20). Both the cloud and the tent cast a shadow. The shadow can be seen but it cannot be touched. Shadow and cloud reveal by concealing and conceal by revealing the indescribable presence of God.

The following reasoning is reached at this point: by putting up their tent amongst us, as the Holy Spirit did to Mary (cf. Luke 1:35) or the Word to Jesus (cf. John 1:14), these divine Persons started to permanently dwell among us. Their dwelling stands for a real and live presence, however mysterious and indescribable it is, which is suggested by the symbolism of the cloud and of the shadow. For instance, when Solomon consecrated the new Temple in Jerusalem it is written that a dark cloud filled the place (cf. 1 Kgs 8:10-13) to symbolize that Yahweh was permanently present there.

Within this framework, to say that Saint Joseph is "the shadow of the Father" means to recognize that the Father inhabits him and that the Father is permanently and consistently present in him. I would say that the Father is personalized in Saint Joseph. But this presence of the Father is not directly announced; rather it is hidden in Joseph. What we see is the father Joseph, but what is hidden in him is the celestial Father. This reasoning enriches our understanding of the Holy Trinity's self-communication to the world. It is not the case that only the Son and the Holy Spirit came amongst us; the Father also came amongst us.

This reasoning also helps us to overcome christocentrism, which breaks the balance of the Trinity. God-Trinity does not self-communicate as parts, but as a whole. The divine Persons devoted themselves to the human persons, and they did this completely and wholly, so that they became personified by human persons. Thus, to state that Joseph is the personification of the Father is to maintain an encompassing understanding. This is what was perceived by a humble but ingenious Franciscan friar, Brother Adauto Schumaker.[8]

---

8. Brother Adauto Schumaker was born on June 30, 1910, in Chopinzinho-Palmas,

SAINT JOSEPH, THE PERSONIFICATION OF THE FATHER

Brother Adauto Schumaker inagurated the fifth and last stage of the theological development relating to Saint Joseph. In a manuscript dated March 19, 1987, the day of the Feast of Saint Joseph, he spells out clearly that Saint Joseph "is the personification of the Father."[9] He was the grandchild of German and Polish immigrates who settled in the south of Brazil, but he opted to live as a Franciscan friar amongst some of the most abandoned people in Brazil, in the Amazonian region of the state of

---

in the state of Paraná, Brazil, and he is of Polish and German extraction. He became a Franciscan in 1927 and was ordained in 1933 in Petrópolis, state of Rio de Janeiro, Brazil. From 1934 to 1952 he worked as a pastoral carer in various parishes, apart from a seven year interval (from 1939 to 1946) when he worked as a typographic proofreader at the Editora Vozes in Petrópolis. From 1952 he moved up north to the state of Maranhão, which is part of the Great Amazon Region, and worked as a parish priest in rural parishes until his death in 2000. Alongside his work with simple people he developed great theological works in connection with cosmology, angelology, Mariology, Josephology, and the doctrine of the Trinity. His writings were very dense and were disseminated around Brazil in the form of photocopies. He was a great devotee of Saint Joseph. He authored a parallel to the *Hail Mary* with the title *Meditation on Saint Joseph: Hail, gracious Saint Joseph; Father God is always with thee; Blessed art thou amongst men; sacred husband of the Virgin Mary; chosen to make way for the Saviour of the world, Jesus; Saint Joseph, father of the People of God; guide our steps in the way of the cross; until the hour of our happy death. Amen.* Beyond his theological works, he invented a method of shorthand that could be applied to all known languages, *Taquigrafia Congruente*, 3 vols. (Rio de Janeiro: Editora Vozes of Petrópolis, 1976–1980).

9. These are manuscripts that were written in pristine calligraphy and which were photocopied and distributed amongst a circle of friends. The first manuscript is titled "Tópicos trinitários"; it is four pages long and is not dated. The second manuscript, "A Trinidade Mediadora—Primícias da Redenção," was written in two very compact pages and it is dated March 19, 1987, and is divided into three parts: i. Mariologia: O Pneuma Personificado, ii. Cristologia: O Filho Personificado, and iii. Josefologia: O Pai Personificado. The third manuscript, which is also two pages long, is titled "A Criação Eterna e a Criação Temporal"; in this manuscript Schumaker lists fourteen expressions of the Trinity—Jesus, Mary, and Joseph being one of these expressions. The fourth manuscript is the most important for the issues I deal with in this book, and it is titled "Josefologia: O Pai Personificado" and is dated March 19, 1987; this manuscript also proposes a modern creed and a short creed. Finally, there is one last manuscript, which is one page long, and is titled " Salve, São José"; it is a prayer to Saint Joseph followed by a litany of Saint Joseph. All these manuscripts are in my possession. Schumaker and I maintained a continuous exchange of ideas through exchanging correspondence and especially when I visited him at Vitorino Freire, a small village in the state of Maranhão, Brazil, which is only reached by travelling four hours on an unpaved road from the town of Bacabal, in July 1978. There, in this village, Schumaker and I reflected together on ideas that were common to both of us.

Maranhão, in the north-eastern region of Brazil, in the town of Bacabal. He was a very forward thinking man and a genius of theorization. His views on creation, evolution, original sin, cosmic function of the angels, and on the mystery of the Holy Trinity went beyond the limits of established dogmas. He went around ridding a horse for days on end in the vast pre-Amazonian forest, a green sea of *babaçu* palm trees, visiting country folk here and there or small villages that are almost inaccessible. When he was doing these visits he had the time to meditate and to give himself up to flights of thinking that he then put into writing and sent to friends. His ideas are very reminiscent of Pierre Teillard de Chardin and are completely trinitarian. He saw triads everywhere. He asserted the divine Trinity (Father, Son, and Holy Spirit), the human trinity (body, soul, and spirit), the terrestrial trinity (Jesus, Mary, and Joseph), the cosmic trinity (proton, electron, and neutron), and some other fourteen trinitarian manifestations. And of particular interest to me in this book is his paper entitled "Josefologia: O Pai personificado," where he maintains that there are three divine humanizations (*hypostasis*): the first through incarnation—Jesus, Son of God; the second through corporality—Mary, God Mother (Holy Spirit); the third through incorporation—Joseph, God Father.[10] After making this point he presents his Josephology. It is more an *insight* than the result of thorough theological reflection, which is what I am trying to do in this book. But there is an extremely fecund element in his intuition: to rescue the architecture and the coherence between the truths of faith. Let me cite the main topics of his Josephology:

> Inter-fusion of Josephology and Patriology. Joseph is God Father humanized, incorporated. Joseph is his eternal Wisdom and Good Sense—which have been incorporated by Joseph, his substitute on earth—at the service of the head of the Holy Family. Joseph is the divine fatherhood shared by the Supreme Father . . . The three of them (Jesus, Mary and Joseph) lived in the sweet peace of the divine love, but also in a constant and excruciating spiritual stress for in the face of the law they were heretics who broke away from the most dear traditions of the chosen people. They submitted themselves and respected the law—circumcision, presentation, purification, annual pilgrimage of Passover—but they interpreted

10. At one of the margins of the document Schumaker wrote: "Which theologian will define these adequately? (Only with the help of angelic inspiration)." He personally challenged me to take up this task, and I am fulfilling this through this book.

these procedures in a different way to others as they were in a painful search for identity. They gradually become aware.[11]

He concludes with this direct interpellation to Saint Joseph: "Joseph, you will cease to be a mere decorative figure of nativity scenes. Your 'protodulia' will be without a doubt VENERATION."[12] The litany of Saint Joseph that he wrote has twenty-four invocations and is, in my opinion, far superior to the official litany which makes excessive use of superlatives, which is something that does not fit well with the humble artisan of Nazareth. The litany written by Brother Adauto Schumaker is discreet. Here are some of the invocations: "Joseph, honored Galilean freeman; humble workman of Nazareth; patron of workmen and artisans; Joseph, sensitive to angelic inspirations; intimate confidant of Mary; educator and confidant of the Child Jesus; Joseph, the personification of God." In his short creed he goes straight to the central point of his views:

> I believe in the God Father omniscient, Creator and Glorifier of heaven and earth, incorporated in Joseph, Father of the Church. I believe in the God Son omnipotent, incarnate in Jesus Christ, Redeemer and Savior of the world, Head and Heart of the Church that is his body. I believe in the Holy Spirit omnipresent, Sanctifier and Mother of universal Creation, embodied in Mary, Mother of the Church. Amen.

This is an explicit and straightforward formulation of the hypostatic relation of the father of Jesus, Joseph, with the celestial Father. The expression *personification* stands for the unrestrained self-communication of the celestial Father to the terrestrial father.

This is a *theologumenon*, that is, a theological thesis that is not official to the Magisterium of the Church nor does it belong to theological tradition. I shall take this thesis on and I shall seek to provide it with an adequate theological formulation. This shall be my collaboration to the intuition of this humble missionary friar who, just as Jesus, did not have a library but an acute sensibility to all things relating to the Spirit.

11. Schumaker, "Josefologia: O Pai personificado," in "A Trindade mediadora—Primícias da redenção," n.p.

12. Translator's note: Dulia (Greek: *doulia*; Latin: *servitus*) is a theological term that stands for the *honor* or *cult* paid to saints. Hyperdulia is a higher sort of honour or cult paid to the Virgin Mary. Protodulia is the honor or cult paid to Saint Joseph and it is placed above dulia but below hyperdulia.

I am aware that my intentions in this book have already a precedent in the seventeenth century works of François-Louis d'Argentan, as I mentioned previously. However, the central thesis of this book only came to the fore in the thought of a Brazilian provincial theologian. I shall take this thesis on and I shall seek to develop it fully.

Apart from this, I shall not engage with anything else other than that which theology is called to do. The Church has always understood that it belongs to theological enquiry to unveil God's intentions. This can be done through revealing God's intentions in the words of the Scriptures or in history, or by reflecting on the symbolisms and analogies of creation, and by always bearing in mind the connections between the many truths of the faith.

To completely fulfill this mission theology cannot become a hostage to its original foundations, nor can theology restrict itself to the Holy Scriptures, to the traditions of the faith, to the ecclesiastical Magisterium, and to established theological reflection. To fulfill this mission theology must encompass all these and go beyond.[13] And it must do this not for mere curiosity but for a sense of mission and of responsibility to bring into light dimensions that are present, but that are still occults, in the mystery of God-Trinity. It is within this context that the personification of the Father in Saint Joseph is found.

Once this task is fulfilled it is only fit for the theologian to say (just as the Gospel says): "We are unworthy servants; we have only done what was our duty" (Luke 17:10).

---

13. The Franciscan Superior said this eulogy when he communicated the death of Brother Adauto Schumaker: "Brother Adauto, a son of God with the courage of being original and not a facsimile, co(s)mic philosopher of calibre and not of a few inconvenient truths, fountain of a thousand happiness and of a few tears, one of our first pioneers in these regions."

8

Saint Joseph of the Father: Personification

I have now reached the central point for my reflections and the main focus of this book; that is, to demonstrate that Saint Joseph is the personification of the celestial Father. In a way I have already prepared the terrain for my reflections in the previous chapter, which dealt with the issue of Saint Joseph belonging to the hypostatic order, and more specifically, with the issue of Saint Joseph as the "shadow of the father," which is to be understood not in a figurative sense, but in a real and ontological sense; finally, in the last chapter I have also dealt with the clear and incisive argument of a Brazilian Franciscan friar concerning the personification of the Father in Saint Joseph.

GOD IS TRINITY AND IT IS REVEALED AS IT IS

Now it is time to recollect all previous points, formulate the thesis, and provide the appropriate theological reasoning. In order to achieve this it is necessary for me before proceeding to clarify two presuppositions that provide support to the thesis and without which the thesis becomes incomprehensible.

The first presupposition says: when God reveals itself, it reveals itself as it is.

It is a conviction present in the whole of the New Testament and in the Christian churches since their beginnings that God is the communion of divine Persons, Father, Son, and Holy Spirit.[1] God is not the

---

1. See the systematic work of Latourelle, *Théology of Revelation*, which is a good source on the issue of revelation; Dulles, *Revelation Theology*; and Moran, *Theology of Revelation* offer a good overview on the issue. A good commentary on the Dei Verbum of the Second Vatican Council that deals with the issue of revelation was written by

solitude of the One but the communion of the Three. At the beginning of everything is this relation. This is the relation that entwined and unites the Persons, so that they are the unique Trinity and not three gods (i.e., the heresy of tritheism). The relation is not something that is posterior to the Persons, but something that happens simultaneously between the Persons. The Persons find themselves eternally and in an essential and original sense always related to each other. Outside this relation there is no Person. The Persons are different so that they can be eternally together and unify themselves in a single God-life-relation-communion-love.[2]

Theology has coined the expression *perichoresis*, which is difficult to translate, to express the insertion of one person in the other, by the other, and with the other, and never without the other. *Perichoresis* stands for the inter-retro-relation of all Persons with all Persons in such an intimate and essential way that it unifies the Persons; that is to say, it turns the Persons into one, it unites them. The Trinity is, thus, a unique God-relation, a unique God-communion, a unique God-love, and a unique God-life.

Hence, when this God-Trinity reveals itself, it reveals itself as a Trinity, that is to say as Father, Son, and Holy Spirit. The Second Vatican Council (1962–65) solemnly stated in the dogmatic constitution *Dei Verbum* that "in his goodness and wisdom God chose to reveal Himself."[3]

Self-revelation implies self-communication. And self-communication occurs when the divine Persons give themselves up without constraints to those whom they decide to be worthy of self-communication. Given the insertion of one Person with another (*perichoresis*), then, when one Person self-communicates it brings with it the other two Persons, preserving the characteristics of each Person. If the Son self-communicates itself to Jesus of Nazareth (incarnation) then it brings with it the Father and the Holy Spirit, despite the fact that only the Son has become incarnate.

To the Christian faith is it not open to discussion that this self-communication took place with Jesus. Jesus is the Son of God incarnate. The

---

Ratzinger (now Pope Benedict XVI), "Das Zweite Vatikanische Konzil"; and for the issue of revelation within the perspective of Latin-American liberation theology see Feller, *O Deus da Revelação*.

2. For the issue of the Holy Trinity see Leonardo Boff, *Trinity*, which includes a detailed bibliography. See also Leonardo Boff, *A Santíssima Trindade*, which is a more compact text.

3. *Dei Verbum*, n. 2.

Son is concretely present in Jesus. In the touching words of Saint John, it is that "which we have heard, which we have seen with our eyes, which we have looked upon and touched with our hands" (1 John 1:1).

The Son brings with it the Father, of whom it is the Son, and the Holy Spirit who formed its humanity ("flesh") in Mary's womb. If this is the case then it is appropriate to ask: Wouldn't that which happened with the Son also happened with the Father? Wouldn't the same also have happened with the Holy Spirit? If one accepts that God-Trinity reveals itself as a Trinity then one can only answer these questions positively. During my life long works in theology I have argued in favor of this kind of well-balanced thinking.

The second presupposition says: the Divine Family, Father, Son, and Holy Spirit, revealed themselves and communicated themselves to the human family of Jesus, Mary, and Joseph.

Just as there is no divine Person in itself and solely for itself but always as a Trinity, then in the same way there is no human person in itself and solely for itself but always as a family. A divine Person does not exist outside the divine Family. A human does not exist outside the human family. In order to understand this implication it is necessary to recover the original and irreplaceable meaning of the family. The family is fundamentally a play of affective relations between people who decide to live together and from whom life emerges. The family is the communion of the father, mother, and son/daughter.

This understanding has nothing to do with the conservative ideology that proposes that the family is disassociated from society as if the family was a perfect oasis far away from the contradictions that are proper to the human condition. This understanding is also disjointed from the understanding of virtual family, the family that emerges from *in vitro* generation. For more technological artifices that are used, one can never generate something out of nothing; rather, generation always requires elements (i.e., semen and egg) whose natural place is the real family. Even if the generation takes place outside the family it is at the bosom of a family relationship that the new being will grow and be educated.

If this is the case with the human family, then with much stronger reasons and through the use of analogy it is also the case with the Divine Family. It is for this reason that the divine self-communication cannot be understood as the exclusive self-communication of one Person without the involvement of the other Persons. If it was not like this, then God would not have self-communicated as it is, that is, as divine Family. The original relation is between families, a relation between the divine Family and the human family.

There is a theological tradition that comes from the Fathers of the Greek Orthodox Church that understood the Holy Trinity as the Divine Family.[4] It established an analogy between the human family and the Divine Family. Just as in the human family is in place at the same time the unity of those with the same nature (i.e., all are human) as well as the differences between the persons (i.e., father, mother, and sons/daughters are all different from each other); in a similar way, in the Divine Family there is a single nature present in the difference of the divine Persons. Also at work is a dynamic movement of life and love in both the human family and Divine Family. The reflection of this theological tradition was limited to this kind of analogy and it never dared to propose the personification of the Divine Family in the human family.

And in accordance with the previously mentioned presuppositions, I argue in favor of the entire self-communication and personification of the Divine Family in the human family. Each of the divine Persons overshadows a particular human person: the Father overshadows Joseph, the Son overshadows Jesus, and the Holy Spirit overshadows Mary.

Coherence and harmony are in place within this kind of thinking. The ultimate purpose of the self-revelation of God-Trinity is realized, which is consonant with the Dogmatic Constitution *Dei Verbum*, n. 2, of the Second Vatican Council: invite human beings—and I would add nature and the entire universe—and take them into fellowship with the divine reality, which is a family-like reality, a communion-like reality that is essentially relational.

If everything in the universe (quantum physicists and contemporary cosmologists tell us), if everything in nature (modern biologists and anthropologists repeat) is a relation because everything is connected to every thing at every point, in every moment and in every circumstance, then everything is a reflection of the Holy Trinity, which is the original relation and source of all real and possible relation.

---

4. For a more detailed discussion see Leonardo Boff, *The Maternal Face of God*, and *Ave Maria*.

These presuppositions provided me with the opportunity to postulate the personification of the celestial Father in the terrestrial father, Saint Joseph.

THE PERSONIFICATION OF THE FATHER IN JOSEPH

I shall seek the appropriate reasoning for my thesis. I shall follow the same path I chose years ago when I wrote my book *The Maternal Face of God*, where I formulated the theological thesis (*theologumenon*) about the personification of the Holy Spirit in Mary.

Firstly, it is important to recognize that in the human being exists the possibility, a concrete disposition, which allows the human being to be taken on by God. This is the human being's nature with infinite projects and unlimited openness to Transcendence. To Christians this possibility and this disposition was activated at the time of the incarnation of the Second Person of the Holy Trinity, the Son, in Jesus of Nazareth. If this provision was not present in the human being then the incarnation would not have been possible.

According to my theological thesis the same occurred with Mary. The Holy Spirit overshadowed her. She said her *fiat* and the Holy Spirit started to permanently dwell in her.

Secondly, the ultimate realization of the human being is only fulfilled when all possibilities, dispositions, and virtualities become fully actualized. This level of plenitude is only possible, in evolutionary terms, when everything in creation and history reaches its full potential, imploding and exploding towards a life of Trinity. Thus, the possibility of being hypostatically taken on by God, a possibility that is present in all human beings, must be fully fulfilled. Each human being will start to belong to God and will be part of its history. Only then will God be "everything to every one" (1 Cor 15:28).

Thirdly, because Saint Joseph is human like us, he possesses this disposition to be taken on by God. Just as the Spirit personified itself in Mary and the Son in Jesus, it is appropriate that Joseph, as husband of Mary and matrimonial father of Jesus, was also taken on by the Father. To God nothing is impossible. Hence, it is fair to say in connection with the personification of the celestial Father in Saint Joseph that *potuit, decuit, ergo fecit!* That is, God could have done it, it was appropriate to have done it, therefore, it was done! Saint Joseph is the personification of the Father.

This statement does not go beyond any other jurisdiction other than that which belongs to theology, as it was set by the First Vatican Council: the mission of theology is to think about the mysteries of God and about everything that is connected to him in the light of "analogy from what it knows naturally, or from the connection of these mysteries with one another and with the final end of humanity."

Fourthly and consonant with this teaching of the Council, the personification of the Father in Joseph represents the highest development in a trend that is confirmed by the Scriptures, that is, the progressive approximation of God to its creation to the point when it invites creation to participate through humanity in its most intimate mystery of life, of communion, and of love.

The theological meaning of creation is to lend itself to the divine purpose, to be a revelation of God itself, of God's goodness, intelligence, and wisdom (cf. Rom 1:20), and to become the precious chalice that receives the good wine of God, that is, God itself when it deigns it appropriate to self-communicate itself.

BIBLICAL CATEGORIES FOR THE DWELLING OF GOD

There are two fundamental biblical categories that express the approximation of God to humanity; moreover, these categories express God's willingness to dwell amongst humanity. These categories are covenant and tent, with the later derivations of the Temple, cloud, and shadow.

Let me first deal with covenant. The covenant was initially with the earth, with life and with the whole of humanity (cf. Gen 9:11–13). Then, the covenant became more concrete with the people of Israel on Mount Sinai (cf. Exod 19:20). The Old Testament is, by and large, the history of the destiny of this covenant, the history of the people's loyal and disloyal relations in their covenant with Yahweh.

In a more advanced phase of the religious consciousness of Israel this covenant was internalized in the heart of each person. Each person must respond directly to God for their loyalty or disloyalty. This is the continuous message of the prophets.

Lastly, the covenant reached its apex when the Holy Spirit overshadowed Mary and the Son overshadowed Jesus. From this moment onwards, God left God's transcendence and entered the depths of human immanence. God left Godself, inviting Godself to a human embrace, and makes Godself human. Such a blessed event is more than a covenant, it is a communion, it is identifying with the other and respecting the differences at the same time. Joseph could not stay outside God's will to incarnate and to personify. The invisible Father becomes visible in Joseph. Joseph could have said something like Jesus said: "The Father is in me and I am in the Father . . . I am in the Father and the Father in me . . . I am the Father are one" (John 10:38; 10:30; 14:11).

The second category is the tent. In the Semitic languages, the tent is the concrete expression of God's dwelling. The resonances of God's dwelling is clear in the words *cloud* and *shadow, tabernacle* and *temple*, which I have previously analyzed. On the one hand these words express the real presence of God who reveals Godself by signs, such as the cloud among the people as it occurred during the crossing of the desert towards the promised land (cf. Exod 40:34–36), or as it occurred during the consecration of Solomon's temple (cf. 1 Kgs 8:10–13). On the other hand, God also veils Godself under the cloak of mystery, for God does not cease to inhabit an inaccessible light. However, the divine presence never leaves the earth, humanity, the people, or each one of the faithful. This is the famous *shekinah*, from which the word *skēnē* is derived, which means "tent" or "dwelling." In Judaism there is the mysticism of the *shekinah*, the undying presence of God in daily life and in the adventures of the people; when happily living in their land, marching towards exile, or being forced into the gas chambers of the Nazi death camps. God never abandons God's people.

The verb "to put the tent up" or "to overshadow" (*skēnoō, episkēnoō*) is the expression that the Scriptures used to translate the self-communication to the maximum of the divine Persons amongst humanity.[5] Hence, Saint Luke uses this word to translate the Holy Spirit's covering Mary in order to dwell permanently in her (cf. Luke 1:35; *episkiasei*). In the same way, Saint John uses this word to express the meaning of the incarnation of the Son, which is to put the tent up amongst humanity (cf. John 1:14; *eskēnōsen*).

5. See the detailed analysis of these verbs in Bauer, *Wörterbuch zum Neuen Testament*, under the entries *skenoo* and *skene*.

Through an analysis of these terms I have understood, with good reasons, why Saint Joseph was called the "shadow of the Father." This shadow is so real that it is equivalent to what I have been clearly saying: Saint Joseph is the "personification of the Father."

At a certain moment in history, when Joseph is faced with Mary's pregnancy by the Holy Spirit, he accepts the situation and decides not to denounce her for adultery, rather, he welcomes her as his true wife, and for this reason welcomes her to his house. At this moment in history, Joseph is not a mere artisan from Nazareth, Mary's fiancé, and a just man; rather, Joseph becomes the human support for this event of infinite blessing: the celestial Father covers his person. From this moment forward the Father will permanently be within humanity. Consequently, we have all been inserted, through Joseph, through Mary, and through Jesus, into the Divine Family.

The consequences of this for our understanding of the mystery of God-Trinity-Relation and of the human condition are immense. And as such, a new area of research is open to theological creativity, to piety, and to the expression of this mystery in human arts.

9

The Divine Family in the Human Family

When one speaks of God-Trinity one must overcome the ambiguities that are present in the concept of *Trinity*. The word suggests the number three, from which Trinity is derived: the three divine Persons, that is, the Father, the Son, and the Holy Spirit. As it happens, God is not numbered. If God is numbered then God is one and unique and not three. The unique is no number, it is rather the negation of number. Thus, the number three of the Trinity must possess a very precise meaning, as I shall demonstrate.

THE HOLY TRINITY IS NOT A NUMBER, IT IS A COMMUNION OF DIFFERENTS

The most important Christian thinker on the Holy Trinity, Saint Augustine (354–430 CE), had already realized that this was a problematic issue. He asked himself: Thus, why speak of a Trinity of Persons? And he answers: because we do not have another way of speaking about that which was manifested in the life of Jesus, and the gospels inform us about the existence of God-Father, God-Son, and God-Holy Spirit.[1]

1. See Saint Augustine *De Trinitate* 7.4.7, where he said: "when it was asked what the three are, which the true faith pronounces to be three, when it both declares that the Father is not the Son, and that the Holy Spirit, which is the gift of God, is neither the Father nor the Son. When, then, it is asked what the three are, or who the three are, we betake ourselves to the finding out of some special or general name under which we may embrace these three; and no such name occurs to the mind, because the super-eminence of the Godhead surpasses the power of customary speech." And in 5.9.10 he adds: "when the question is asked, What three? human language labors altogether under great poverty of speech. The answer, however, is given, three " persons," not that it might be [completely] spoken, but that it might not be left [wholly] unspoken."

Saint Augustine emphasizes that God does not multiply itself as if Father, Son, and Holy Spirit are three different gods (tritheism). God is solely one and it is unique. Saint Augustine continuously repeated: "the One and only and true God, the Trinity itself," or, "therefore, is God Himself, the Trinity."[2] In order to reach a minimum understanding about what it is that is intended to express with the concept *Trinity* it is necessary to put aside for a moment one's conventional way of seeing things. Normally we see things statically, we see things as objects placed side-by-side and susceptible to enumeration. If one follows this same way of thinking in relation to the Holy Trinity then the Trinity is simply understood as a number ($1+1+1=3$). There would not even be a reason to stop at three, one could go to infinity, as the philosopher Immanuel Kant ironically, but erroneously, observed.[3]

One can, however, see things in a different way: dynamically, always related to one another, associating in unions, and establishing communion and ties of participation. This is, in fact, the logic of the universe, of nature, of life, as modern cosmology (i.e., understanding of reality) has systematically maintained: nothing exists outside relations, everything is inter-retro-connected with everything, constituting a complex and awesome web of inclusion.

If one wants to achieve some understanding of the Holy Trinity one must thus take on this way of thinking and of seeing the world. Suddenly, one discovers relations and realizes that everything is relation. The employed terminology itself already presupposes relations: there is no Father without a Son, nor Son without a Father. There is no Breath (this is the meaning of Holy Spirit) without someone breathing. The Holy Spirit is the Breath of the Father into the Son and the Breath of the Son into the Father.

The number three of Trinity is not a mathematical number by which one can add, deduct, or multiply, for the Unique-Ones cannot be put together because they are singular. The number three is still a number, but it now becomes a symbol and an archetype, which is found in all cultures of the world. The number three stands for the unity in difference and the difference in unity. This understanding was convincingly noted by one of

2. Saint Augustine, *De Trinitate*, 1.6.10–11.

3. See *Der Streit der Fakultäten*, Berlin: 1917, 38–39. Available in English as *The Conflict of Faculties*.

the fathers of psychoanalysis, C. G. Jung.[4] The archetypal three expresses a perfect and complete relation. Let me demonstrate this.

If there were only the one then there would be solitude and lack of communication. If there were only the two then there would be separation (one is distinct from the other) and exclusion (one is not the other), and there would be a face-to-face relation between them in a narcissistic contemplation. When the three appears it opens up the possibility of the different, of openness, the possibility for the two to look outside of themselves and in the direction of the third. The three does away with solitude, it overcomes separation and it overrides exclusion. The three asserts the identity (the Father), it is open to the different (the Son), and it allows for communion (the Holy Spirit).

I emphasize that the three does not stand for the mathematical number within this context, it rather stands for the understanding that under the concept God there are differences that are not exclusive but inclusive, that are not opposing but in communion. The defining feature here is the union through relation, communion, and love.

It is for this reason that I have written in various passages of this book that at the beginning there is not the solitude of the One, but the communion of the Three: the Father, the Son, and the Holy Spirit. They emerge simultaneously and in relation to one another. They co-exist eternally inside one another, for one another, with one another, and never without the other. The great theologian Saint John of Damascus (ca. 676–750) expressed this well when he wrote: "it is just like three suns cleaving to each other without separation and giving out light mingled and conjoined into one."[5] Trinity stands for this circulation of life, of inclusion and of love.

Our culture is founded on segmentation and atomization, and it sees each single thing as something in itself disconnected and isolated from other things. For this reason, our culture becomes blind to the inter-relations and inter-dependences that give rise to the perception of a dynamic and encompassing whole. By being inserted and educated within this

4. Jung, "A Psychological Approach to the Dogma of the Trinity."

5. John of Damascus *De fide orthodoxa* I.8, n. 14; It is worth mentioning also Saint Gertrude (1256–1302) who described a trinitarian vision she had: "the three Persons irradiated an awesome light: each one of them seemed to launch its own flame through the others causing each person to merge with one another"; cited by Oehl, *Deutsche Mystiker* II, 39.

dominant paradigm, Christians find it very difficult to understand the discourse on the Holy Trinity. And the theology that is embedded in modern culture finds it difficult to break away from this limitation and shows little interest in reflecting upon the Holy Trinity. And, when theology tries to do this, it produces arguments that are extremely formal and abstract, which turns these arguments practically inaccessible to the vast majority of Christians.

To sum up: if I say that God is the eternal communion of the different, I am in essence stating that which I want to say with the expression Holy Trinity.

THE HOLY TRINITY IS THE DIVINE FAMILY

The fact that the Father, the Son, and the Holy Spirit always live together in an eternal play of love and of giving oneself to the other allows me to say that God is thus a family, a Divine Family. In fact, Pope John Paul II said this to the gathering of all Latin American bishops in Puebla, Mexico, on January 28, 1979, the occasion of his first visit to Latin America, and I personally heard him stating: "It has already been said in a beautiful and profound manner that our God, in its intimate mystery, is not solitude but a family for it bears within itself the paternity, the affiliation and the essence of the family, which is love; in the Divine Family this love is the Holy Spirit."[6]

This statement is relevant and absolutely correct, for the Holy Trinity concretizes within the infinite realm that which we perceive in our experience of the human family.

Firstly, the family is the co-existence of unity and of difference. There are different persons: the father, the mother, and the sons/daughters; all of them are different, but they form a unique family. It is the same with the Divine Family: the divine Persons are different, but all of them are the unique and holy Trinity.

Secondly, as was emphasized by John Paul II in his Apostolic Exhortation, *Familiaris Consortio* of 1981, the family is "a complex of interpersonal relations."[7] In a similar way the Holy Trinity is fundamentally simultaneous and eternal inter-personal relations.

6. Translator's note: Boff refers here to the Third Conference of Latin American Bishops (CELAM III), which was held in Puebla, Mexico, 1979.

7. John Paul II, *Familiaris Consortio*, n. 15; see also John Paul II, *Letter to Families*, where the same idea occurs.

Thirdly, that which governs these inter-personal relations is the love between all the members, father-mother-sons/daughters, and which unites the family. In the Trinity love is the link uniting all the Persons and that compels them to uni-fy (i.e., become one) into only one God-love. It is love, as was rightly said by Saint Augustine, that allows for each of the Persons of the Holy Trinity to be "each . . . in each, and all in each, and each in all, and all in all, and all are one."[8]

Fourthly, the love within the family turns the family into a community of persons living the communion of all and the sharing in everything that concerns everybody. Analogously, the Holy Trinity is "the best community," as per the motto held by the representatives of the Comunidades Eclesiais de Base de todo o Brasil (Ecclesial Community-Base), gathering in the central region of Brazil, in the small town of Trindade, state of Goiás, in July 1986. The communion and the sharing between the divine Persons compels them to be a eternal community, a Divine Family.

This overcomes the bad habit of individualism, which is inherent to Western culture, which sees each of the Persons set apart, and which does not perceive the essential relation that each Person has with the others.

In short, that which there is in reality is the Trinity, which is the Family of Persons. Equally, that which there is in reality is the human family, which is also formed by persons.

As I shall demonstrate later, even if the format of the family varies in accordance with cultures and times, and even if the classical conceptualization of the family finds itself transformed by the changes in our modern times, the rationality behind the family does not change. The family is the natural and proper place for the concrete constitution of our humanity. At least the essential elements of the family remain, namely, fatherhood and motherhood. Even if there is artificial procreation outside the wedlock with the aid of technology, a human being is never "produced." The human being is not "produced," it rather "comes into the world" in the heart of a social community where it requires love and care to live and to survive humanely.

THE DIVINE FAMILY PERSONIFIES ITSELF IN THE HUMAN FAMILY

This Divine Family willed to come out of itself, to leave its indescribable transcendence and mysteriousness, and to invite another family to take

8. Augustine *On the Holy Trinity* 6.10.12.

communion and participate in its unutterable intimate life. Hence, the Divine Family gave itself totally up to a human family.

This family is the humble family of Nazareth, the family of Joseph, Mary, and Jesus. This human family was taken on by, and became part of, the Divine Family. This event of infinite divine and human gentleness occurred more than two thousand years ago, far away from the gaze of the great of this world, in a hidden corner of this world, in a working family in simple and poor conditions but embedded in piety and unction, in the family of Jesus, Mary, and Joseph. This family stands for all human families of all times and cultures. All families, under different names and interpretations, take part in this personification.

In some way, the celestial Trinity prepared this family to become the terrestrial trinity. Within this family is Mary, who is called by the gospels as "favored one" (Luke 1:28) and "blessed are you among women" (Luke 1:42); within this family is Joseph, who is called "just man" (Matt 1:19); within this family is Jesus, who "increased in wisdom and in stature, and in favor with God and man" (Luke 2:52).

To their neighbors' glance they constituted a normal family with close relations with their relatives (cf. Luke 1:39–80). To the Trinity's glance this represents the discreet and silent entrance of the Divine Family into the human family, so to enable all families to take part in its communion and eternal life.

This perspective radicalizes that which Christians believe and which is clearly written in the *Catechism of the Catholic Church* (1993): the "family is a symbol and an image of the community of the Father and of the Son in the Holy Spirit" (n. 2205). This is to be understood as not only the Christian family, but all human family, and religion and time are of no concern here. The family of Nazareth becomes, through the coming of the Holy Family into it, more than a mere symbol and an image. This is the historical embodiment of the community of the Father in the Son through the Holy Spirit in the community of Joseph, Mary, and Jesus.

It is important to emphasize here this communitarian and inclusive side of the Trinity's self-communication before proceeding with my argument on the personification of each of the divine Persons: the Father in Joseph, the Son in Jesus, and the Holy Spirit in Mary. In this way, I shall maintain the trinitarian and communitarian character of the Christian way of nominating God, which is always connected with the communion of the Persons as a Community and as a Divine Family.

The incarnation of the Son in our brother Jesus of Nazareth has touched all human beings and also the whole of the universe (because we are made of the same elements that form the various bodies of the universe), as we were reminded in the Second Vatican Council.[9] In the same way the personification of the Divine Family in the human family touched all human families. The human family gained a mark that it did not possess before, it gained a singular relation with each of the divine Persons.

Through the human family the biotic community, of which we are just a link, was also affected. The terrestrial and cosmic community itself, the great family of all beings on earth and in the universe, which are all inter-linked and inter-dependent, were inserted into this process of personification. Something of the universe started to belong to God-Trinity via the holy family of Nazareth; but in a way, it was already inserted into the Kingdom of the Trinity, which is the ultimate destination of all creation.

A DYNAMIC AND TENSE REALITY

How did the holy family of Nazareth experience this intimate relation with the Divine Family? Certainly, it did not experience this relation in the same terms I have been speaking. We have inherited more than two thousand years of theological reflection through which we express, by the use of concepts that are inherent in our culture, Jesus' and the holy family's experiences. This experience was that they felt themselves involved in something that was very mysterious: Mary with the Holy Spirit, which made her pregnant; Jesus with the Son, which became incarnate in him; and Joseph, the terrestrial father, with the celestial Father, with whom he felt himself to be in a profound communion. The reality of the Holy Trinity was in action here, even if they did not have the words to express this reality, as we do. They did not even need to be aware of the Holy Trinity's action, because what is important is not their conscious reflection on the action, but what the Holy Trinity objectified in their lives.

Certainly, one must allow for the fact that there must have been some sort of awareness that what was happening had a strong connection with God itself. But this was an awareness gained through experience and not through intellectual formulation, as I am currently doing.

9. See *Gaudium et Spes*, n. 22.

This awareness could have developed further, as is common to the evolutionary human process. The gospel texts suggest this further development, which can encompass a feeling of amazement and of bewilderment. One could say: the members of the family of Nazareth, Jesus, Mary, and Joseph, each of them departing from their singular positions and within the play of inter-relations that were normally established between them in their daily lives as a family, helped each other to further increase their awareness of the Holy Trinity's action.

Two facts have been revealed to us: first, the encounter of Jesus in the Temple, after he failed to join the caravan to Nazareth (cf. Luke 2:41–52), with Mary and Joseph, who as any normal parents worried and reproached their child. The child replied in an unexpected way that caused them to reflect: "Did you not know that I must be in my Father's house?" (Luke 2:49). With this statement Jesus reveals a state of awareness more developed with reference to his singular relation with the celestial Father. Luke comments: "And they did not understand the saying which he spoke to them" (Luke 2:50). But Jesus' statement must have certainly provided Mary and Joseph with food for thought and in this way forced them to grow. Indeed, Luke says something about Mary that is most certainly also true of Joseph: Mary "kept all these things in her heart" (Luke 2:51). This kind of relationship, which is tense and not easy, allowed them to develop their awareness about their involvement with God.

The second fact, which is in a way a bit scandalous for pious ears, occurred right at the beginning of Jesus' public life. He left home, of his own accord, and started to preach around Galilee. Saint Mark, the oldest evangelist and the evangelist who preserved most historical facts, said that Jesus' parents went after him because Jesus brought shame on them and that because of this they wanted to bring him back. Saint Mark writes: "He is beside himself" (Mark 3:21). And elsewhere it is written: "Your mother and your brothers are outside, asking for you . . . Who is my mother, and who are my brothers? And stretching out his hand toward his disciples, he said, 'here are my mother and my brothers!' . . . My mother and my brothers are those who hear the word of God and do it." (Mark 3:31–35; Matt 12:46–50; Luke 8:19–21).

The lesson to be learned here is about the affirmation of a new kind of extended family that emerges through the faith of Jesus' preaching, and it has nothing to do with Mary and the other relatives of Jesus being undermined in any way whatsoever. This new extended family transcends conventional blood ties. Faith founds a new community, faith which Jesus' mother exemplarily showed during the annunciation when she said "yes" to the angel, and this is something that was praised by her cousin Elizabeth, who said: "And blessed is she who believed that there would be a fulfillment of what was spoken to her from the Lord" (Luke 1:45).

Hence, an unevenness is noticeable between Jesus' awareness and the awareness of Mary's and Jesus' other relatives. Once more, this fact must have aided Mary and the other relatives to grow in awareness about the mystery that embraced them.

Moreover, the fact that the Divine Family personifies itself in the human family of Jesus, Mary, and Joseph does not interfere with the limitations of the sciences and the limitations of consciousness that are inherent to the human condition. The important issue is not what the human family thinks and is of aware in its subjectivity. The important issue is rather what the Divine Family achieves, within the human limitations that it takes up, in the family of Nazareth. The personification is a process that accompanies the various phases and situations of the terrestrial family. The Divine Family takes up the terrestrial family to the extent in which these various phases and situations occur.

A correct theology of incarnation teaches that the Word takes up the human nature to the extent that human nature manifests itself, with all the blemishes, except sin, that it possesses. When Saint John says "the Word became flesh" (John 1:14), with the term *flesh* he wants to express the limited human situation, which is full of sufferings and mortal. It is in this flesh (and not in spite of the flesh) that the Word decided to dwell permanently. This same reasoning is valid for the Divine Family's personification in the human family.

This realistic understanding overturns that static, lyric, and naive conception found in pious and edifying texts. This realistic understanding invites us to think dialectically about the relation between the Divine Family and the human family. Step by step, the human family was being taken up with its bewilderments, with its embarrassments, with its long silences, with its discreet moments of joy and of satisfaction, for all these are common to the human family. Thus, it is not *in spite of these issues*, it is rather *with these issues* that the indescribable assumption of the human family by the Divine Family took place.

10

The Celestial Father in the Terrestrial Father

The heavenly Divine Family personifies itself in the terrestrial holy family. In this chapter I want to consider in detail the personification of the Father in father Joseph. There must have been connaturality between them, there must have been reasons for the Father to completely self-communicate to father Joseph, and to do this only to him.

The initiative to take up the person of Joseph was the Father's in his unutterable goodness and affection. If this is the case then I must, before proceeding, seek to understand better who the Father is. The best way to do this is to investigate what the incarnate Son communicated to us about his eternal Father.[1] The Son revealed to us the being of the Father, the doings of the Father, and the way in which the Father establishes a relation. Let me demonstrate these in detail.

THE BEING, THE DOING, AND THE RELATING OF THE FATHER

The Gospels of the New Testament state clearly that: "[God] dwells in unapproachable light, whom no man has ever seen or can see." (1 Tim 6:16). Or "No one has ever seen God; the only Son, who is in the bosom of the Father, he has made him known" (John 1:16; cf. 6:46; 1 John 4:12). And Jesus himself clearly said: "no on knows the Father except the Son and any one to whom the Son chooses to reveal him" (Matt 11:27). The Father is invisible and an enigmatic mystery, a principle without a principle. Before him silence is appropriate for any word would be chatter.

1. On this subject, see, for instance: Jeremias, *Abba*; Durrwell, *Le Père*; L. Bouyer, *Le Père Invisible*; P. Galot, " Pour une Théologie du Père"; Le Guillou, *Il Mistero del Padre*; Leonardo Boff, *O Pai-Nosso and Trinity*; various authors, *Il Mistero del Padre*; see also *Concilium* 163 (1981).

For this reason one can speak of the silence of the Father. His Word is the Son.

However, this mystery of enigmatic silence is not threatening, but fascinating because it is an abyss of love, tenderness, and welcome. This is revealed by Jesus when he calls the Father by using a word that reflects infinite intimacy and tenderness: 'Abba, my dear Daddy.

This way of speaking reflects the intimate love of the Son towards the Father, and this goes to the extent of Jesus saying the following, which resembles a lover's speech: "I and the Father are one" (John 10:30); or "all mine are thine, all thine are mine" (John 17:30). And consequently, "He who has seen me has seen the Father" (John 14:9). Therefore, it is through the Son that the being of the Father becomes visible and accessible to us (cf. John 1:18; 14:9). Otherwise, the Father would remain in eternal silence.

This is the being of the Father, but it is through his doings that the Father is even more revealed. The silence is operational, it is the silence of one who works and creates. The doings of the Father is a model for the doings of Jesus: "the Son can do nothing of his own accord, but only what he sees the Father doing" (John 5:19). Doing is a work of the hand and not of the mouth.

The doing of the Father is in favor of his sons and daughters to whom he shows his merciful love, his unconditional embrace of the prodigal child, and his preference for the poor and marginalized. If Jesus says, "Blessed are you poor, for yours is the kingdom of God" (Luke 6:20), he says this not merely in a humanitarian sense but in virtue of the Father's bias for them: "For as the Father raises the dead and gives them life, so also the Son gives life to whom he will" (John 5:21). Jesus does not preach any doctrine about the Father, he rather does what the Father does. For this reason, Jesus cures, re-evaluates the rules of the law, overlooks the sacred Sabbath, walks around accompanied by people with doubtful reputation to demonstrate the Father's mercy, forgive sins, and resurrects the dead. And Jesus concludes: "My Father is working still, and I am working" (John 5:17).

The work of the Father is subtle, it is only perceived by those who have eyes of faith. Indeed the Father's caring actions can be seen in the lilies of the field, with the birds of the air, with each hair in our head, and with simple human necessities such as eating and clothing (cf. Matt 6:26–32).

The Father's greatest work, which Jesus took on as a mission, was the definitive establishing of the Father's Kingdom. The Kingdom of the God-Father is not a conventional kingdom of the powerful that is imposed through domination. The Kingdom of God is a new way of being for things and a new state of consciousness for people. The Kingdom, which is in the midst of us (cf. Luke 17:21), is that state of things and people that arises when goodness, love, compassion, and the rights of the poor prevails in them; it is that state when the whole of creation starts to be freed, when diseases are cured, when sins are forgiven and when death is conquered. This Kingdom is implemented to the extent that people engage themselves in this auspicious proposal, the Gospel. The Kingdom is ongoing, it is always open and it always moves forward in the form of hope, as an object of a continuous plea: "Thy kingdom come" (Luke 11:2; Matt 6:10).

Lastly, attributed to the Father is the creation of the heavens and earth, as we pray in the Christian creed. We know that due to the Trinitarian communion all the divine Persons take part in creation. But it belongs to the concept of the Father "to generate" and to create, despite of the fact that he always does this alongside the Son and with the power of the Holy Spirit. As a Father it creates and as a Mother it cares. For this reason the Father is maternal and the Mother is paternal.[2] Everything in him is enveloped in love, wisdom, symmetry, order, creativity, as it can be seen in the logic of the universe and of life. The existing chaos itself is not chaotic, but a source of new orders and complexities.

The Father let his voice be heard when he said of his Son Jesus: "This is my beloved Son, with whom I am well pleased" (Matt 3:17). This is a message that Christians believe to be said about each son and daughter that comes into this world. The Father's love is directed to all, it does not matter the moral standing of the person, for it embraces and forgives the prodigal child just as a loving Mother would do (cf. Luke 15:11–32), it provides sun and rain to just and unjust and continues to love the ungrateful and the wicked (cf. Matt 5:45). Jesus' tenderness towards all employed the infinite love of the Father: "All that the Father gives me will come to me; and him who comes to me I will not cast out" (John 6:36). Jesus, mirroring the Father, welcomed all: the Pharisees who plotted against him and who invited him for a meal; an embarrassed theologian,

---

2. See Leonardo Boff, *Trinity*; Moltmann, "The Motherly Father"; L. M. Almendariz, "El Padre Maternal."

Nicodemus; the children; a Samaritan woman; the Lepers who called him from afar: "Lord, cure-us."

THE FATHER IS FATHER OF THE SON
BEFORE BEING THE CREATOR

The Father is Father because he has alongside him the Son and the Holy Spirit. In both the New Testament and in the official discourse of the ecumenical councils of the Church it is stated that the Father eternally "generates" the Son and "exhales" with the Son or through the Son the Holy Spirit. In this way, he is Father before being Creator. Through creating, he makes himself Father of all beings. But, even if he had not created anything the Father would have been Father because he eternally "generates" the Son and "exhales" the Holy Spirit.

The expressions *generate* and *exhale* must be understood in an analogical, rather than physical, sense. Otherwise, these expressions can lead us to an erroneous understanding of the Holy Trinity. *To generate* seems to presuppose that the Father comes before, that the Father is the cause of the Son, just as one's father comes before and generates a child. If this was the case then there would be a sort of *theogony* in God, that is to say, a process through which the Persons would derive themselves one from another, would come into being and would come into the light.

Within the Trinitarian reflection this cannot be the case because within it everything is eternal and simultaneous. No one is prior or after, there are no hierarchies. The divine persons emerge together and simultaneously, always inter-related amongst themselves. The Council of Toledo (675) taught: "the Son was born, but not made, from the substance of the Father, without beginning, before all ages, for at no time did the Father exist without the Son, nor the Son without the Father." And the same is said about the Holy Spirit, as was emphasized by the Fourth Lateran Council (1215): "the Holy Spirit . . . eternally without beginning or end . . . co-substantial and co-equal, co-omnipotent and co-eternal."[3]

Due to the ambiguity of the expressions *generate* and *exhale* many theologians prefer to use the word *revelation*: the Father reveals the Son, and the Son reveals the Father; and both when they give themselves up reveal the Holy Spirit.

---

3. "The Canons of the Fourth Lateran Council," Canon 1.

One must acknowledge, however, that the terms *generation* and *exhale* are highly suggestive. These expressions have an internal relational logic, for to say Father, Son, and Holy Spirit (Breath) is to state the difference and the inter-relation at the same time. The Father will always be the Father of the Son, the Son will eternally be the Son of the Father, with the same nature of the Father and in infinite communion with him. The Holy Spirit (Breath) will always be and has always been the gift of the Father and of the Son. The Word (Son) that is said by the Father is always accompanied by the Breath (the Holy Spirit).

This circle of communion and of love is not closed in on itself. It opens itself up to communion with the universe as an expression of the superabundance of the life and of the love of the Trinity. The divine Persons come out of themselves and give themselves up to the human persons Joseph, Mary, and Jesus.

JOSEPH, TERRESTRIAL FATHER WHO IS CONNATURAL TO THE CELESTIAL FATHER

In Joseph of Nazareth, in the artisan-carpenter, in the husband of Mary and in the father of Jesus, the Father found the person who was connatural to him, and he decided to personify Himself in him.

The Father is invisible. Joseph is equally invisible, which is consonant to the texts of the New Testament. Joseph is invisible all along the centuries of Christian history. And the veils that covered his mystery were lifted very slowly. But he continuous to be invisible. And he will certainly remain as such because this is in accordance with his nature and mission: to personify the invisible Father. Joseph Ephraïm, a well-known Josephologist, writes: "The Father, invisible mystery in person, incomprehensible in its being and works, chose Joseph to be his image on Earth: for this reason Saint Joseph is also invisible-like and hidden from our spirits."[4]

The Father is an enigmatic silence. Joseph is the prototype of silence. Joseph did not leave us a single word, he only left us dreams. His speech is not through words, but through the attitudes, deeds, and commitments of a father and husband. He gives body to the silence of the Father.

The Father is the "artisan" of the universe, as the Fathers of the Latin and Greek churches used to say, for he created, together with the Son

4. Ephraïm, *Joseph*, 108.

and the Holy Spirit, all things in heaven and earth. Joseph is an artisan-carpenter who worked in his workshop having Jesus at his side in Nazareth, and probably in the town of Sepphoris, which is close by and which was being rebuilt on Roman orders. To work is to establish a positive relation with creation, it is to transform creation to fulfill our necessities, it is to take care of creation for we are its guardians and gardeners, as it is clearly said in the book of Genesis (cf. Gen 2:15). The Father works through the works of Joseph. As it is normally the case, the work represents the universe of anonymous people, the world of normal daily lives in which the vast majority of humanity lives, a world that is not publicized but that is essential for production and generation of life, and a privileged place for human self-realization. The Father, personified in Joseph, penetrated this realm; and his Son Jesus did the same for through incarnation he took up all the possibilities and limitations of the human condition. The Father takes care of creation and of each son and daughter. Joseph also took care of the holy family during the various moments of their experiences. Joseph made sure, through his work, that his wife and son had all their needs met.

The intimate relation between Jesus and the celestial Father demonstrated by Jesus' use of the word 'abba is derived, as it is argued by religious psychology, from the experiences he lived with his terrestrial father Joseph. Curiously, the experiences converge and become one: the celestial Father is found in the terrestrial father.

WAS SAINT JOSEPH AWARE THAT HE WAS THE PERSONIFICATION OF THE FATHER?

It was not required that Jesus consciously lived this experience and perceived Joseph to be the personification of the Father for this experience to be validated. For this, it is enough that Jesus lived to the full his relation with the celestial Father and with his terrestrial father.

This is achieved in a single movement, just as in the case of loving God and loving your neighbor, which is at the heart of a single commandment, the commandment of love (cf. Matt 22:37–40). One experience awakens the other so that Jesus felt himself to be truly Son of the Father and, at the same time, son of Joseph.

The same can be said regarding Joseph as the personification of the Father within this line of thought. It was not required of him to consciously live this historic fact of salvation, and anyway this is difficult to assert given that he did not leave us a single written word. But there are other ways to assert one's level of awareness. One such way is through one's daily life experiences.

If we pay close attention we become aware that the most important events in our life do not occur at a conscious level, but at the deepest level of the act of living itself. This act of living has roots in ancestral, cosmic, biological, human and personal memories, which characterized for being largely unconscious, partly subconscious and only a tiny bit conscious. Our blood runs through our veins, our heart beats, our digestive system functions without passing through our consciousness. The biological-material basis of our rationality resides in the billions and billions of neurons and in the trillions and trillions of synapses and connections that are established between the neurons. Nevertheless, we think and feel without having the minimum experience and conscience about this fantastic work of our brains. The Earth spins around itself and it moves through space at great speed. And we are neither aware nor do we feel any of this.

What do we know about our lives? Who are we ultimately serving? What is the larger context into which we are inserted as part and parcel? These issues that are fundamental to our living escape our consciousness. However, these issues still take place in us and through us.

For this reason we must re-evaluate subjectivity, which is greatly overrated in our modern Western culture. Its scope of realization and action is limited. Hindu sages said a long time ago: "the powers through which the mind thinks is not thought." Or in a more modern formulation: "the eye sees everything but it cannot see itself," for "the eye that sees the world is the world that the eye sees."

Hence, if this is the case, one is entitled to say that the power through which Joseph is the personification of the Father transcends consciousness. The important thing is the fact that Joseph was a complete father, Joseph consciously fulfilled all the tasks that are proper to a father, Joseph was a father who entertained an intimate relation with God and Joseph gave himself up to him in unconditional trust. When Saint Matthew says that Joseph was "a just man" (Matt 1:19) it is implicit that Joseph did everything that he needs and had to do exemplarily. This way of being is an expression of the presence of the Father in his life as a father, husband, and worker.

We are not only connected to God through our full consciousnesses; rather we are connected to God through the totality of our being, through our unconscious, subconscious, conscious mind, and its various dimensions, its cosmic, biological, vegetal, animal, human, racial, familiar and personal dimensions. All these dimensions were taken up by the Father when he personified himself in the person and in the concrete life of Joseph of Nazareth.

11

The Family in the Light of the Holy Family

Before schematically tackling the complex issue of the family it is imperative to deal with another issue, without which all my reflections in this
book would appear to be flawed or condemned to be a utopia. This is the
issue that the family, more than any other reality, shares those ambiguities that are inherent to the human condition, ambiguities that make us
simultaneously *demens* and *sapiens*, sym-bolic and dia-bolic; in short,
these ambiguities reveal us as a living co-existence of contradictions.
Thus, on the one hand the family encapsulates the highest of values, and
on the other hand it includes lamentable distortions. And following on
from this, living in family is a permanent conflict, with opportunities to
face challenges and for growth, but also with the risk of decadence and of
the situation deteriorating.

FAMILY: UTOPIA AND REALITY

Nevertheless the utopian dimension does not disappear from us. We re-
fuse to passively accept a situation of decadence. We want to overcome
it. We do not second a lazy pragmatism without dreams and we are not
destitute of a will for improvement, a lazy pragmatism that only adminis-
trates the crisis, taking advantage whenever it can, but without a project
of generating new models of living together. Unfortunately, this is the
dominant trend, particularly within the context of postmodernity where
anything goes and where value is placed on *what is in fashion*.

A person or a society, however, that does not dream anymore and
that does not guide itself according to the utopias has chosen a pathway
of decadence that will lead to its disappearance. Without utopia it is im-

possible to feed hope. Without hope there is no reason to continue to live, and the fatal outcome is self-destruction. For this reason the utopian dimension is of extreme importance in everything we undertake, no less with respect to the family, and even if we are aware that we will never achieve this utopia. However, the utopian dimension has an irreplaceable role because it re-evaluates historic-social issues and maintains an open future. In short, utopia keeps us moving. We will never reach the stars, but what would be of the night without these? It is the stars that frighten away the ghost of darkness and that fill us with reverence when faced with the grandiosity and majesty of the heavens.

Therefore, there is a need for a utopia for the family, so that it continues to be human, so that it is a place of fulfillment for the love and trust of two people, so that it is worthy of generating new lives for the universe and for God.[1]

When we compare the human family to the divine Family and the holy family of Nazareth, however, all those aforementioned contradictions become obvious. There is a risk here of falling into a one-sided kind of discourse: on the one hand to praise the excellences of the divine Family and of the holy family of Nazareth, and on the other hand to point out the various blemishes of the human family, instead of elaborating a proper comparison between them.

Another risk, which often appears in the documents of the Magisterium of the Church and in sermons at churches, is to present from the pulpit the utopia of the Christian family without taking seriously the challenges that come from real families, which face changing pressures of all kinds. Hence, the official discourse is unrealistic for it does not address the real needs of Christians. My discourse, even if brief, seeks to maintain the dialectics between utopia and the contradictory real, starting from the challenges of the real and then confronting it with the utopian. In this way, I hope to do justice to these two dimensions and in doing so I hope to provide a space for inspirations that stimulate creativity within the historic-social context in which we suffer and live.

1. The bibliography concerning the family and matrimony is endless. The following texts are a good sources on the subject: *Concilium* 55 (1970) and 260 (1995); Bach, *O Futuro da Família*; Schillebeeckx, *Marriage*; Vidal, *Moral do Matrimônio*; E. B. Moreira de Azevedo and L. M. Moreira de Azevedo, *Matrimônio*; CNBB, *Casamento e família no mundo de hoje*; Leonardo Boff, "O sacramento do Matrimônio."

THE FAMILY AND HISTORIC-SOCIAL TRANSFORMATIONS

The family suffers greatly from the impact of the dominant culture, which is now globalized. The dominant culture is characterized by social processes that place the economy as the structural axis of everything. The economy and its major instrument, the market, have as its central rule fierce competition, which pushes aside values such as cooperation and solidarity, which are so essential to human life and to the family. The dominant culture has brought undeniable benefits to the human condition but it has also aggravated it because it is more interested in offering material goods than anything else. Non-material values that are connected to gratuity, to love, to solidarity, to fraternity, to exchange, and to spirituality occupy an irrelevant place, except when these are turned into commodities to be sold in the market.

The family lives off these values. And this means that our culture does not offer sufficient conditions for the family to live in normal circumstances and to live its dreams. Moreover, our culture destroys the infrastructure that the vast majority of families need to subsist, to experience love and to take care for its sons/daughters. This is so because the accumulation of wealth is very uneven. This globalized social injustice gives rise to millions and millions of impoverished families, which are marginalized and excluded. Separations and divorces are on the rise. The main victims of these are young children, to whom the essential conditions of the first three formative years are negated, when they elaborate through their contact with the mother and later with the father the basic dispositions that will guide them throughout their whole lives: these are the feelings of belonging, the understanding of care, protection, and other essential values that provide direction in life.

As one may gather, this kind of social organization does not stand up to instigating values, nor does it take into account collective ethical criteria that go beyond individual interests. The spiritual dimension becomes something private or is presented within this social organization in a very anemic form. Such an atmosphere does not encourage a favorable environment for a well-integrated and well-rounded family, nor does it induce motivations to resist the generalized erotic appeals of the present forms of communication, which debilitate the ties of fidelity and conjugal affection, nor does it offer help in moments of crises.

To this dramatic family scenario can be added the profound social and technological changes that greatly affect the family status. The traditional forms of the family are about to disappear.

The classical family, centered around the figure of the father, who distributed family roles according to gender, which privileged the husband and father, is giving way to a participative family, where the husband and wife take on all tasks within a cooperative framework, and this is an aspect that must be positively valued.

What is emerging today as the result of the acceleration of the urbanization process in the world is the nuclear family of father/mother and sons/daughters. This kind of family subcontracts functions that before were proper to the family because of the couple's work regime, i.e., both work outside the family home. The baby is cared for by a nanny or housemaid, and later it is looked after at a crèche; the house is tidied up, meals are prepared, and the care of the elderly or sick are subcontracted. Only the inter-subjective relations of affection and companionship are left to the couples.

The extended family, which encompasses all blood ties, tend to be diluted especially in the great cities. The greater family, which included all those who lived under the same roof, family members, relatives, lodgers, and maids, is now practically only seen in respect to great plantation owners who live in archaic family relations.

The old families restrict themselves to some form of noble title. They tend to cultivate traditions and maintain family memories, but in general they do this in a conservative and social elitist way.

CHALLENGES TO NEW MODES OF CO-HABITATION

Alongside married families, which are constituted under the judicial-social and sacramental framework, we increasingly see the emergence of partnership-families (i.e., co-habitation and partnerships) that are constituted consensually outside the institutional framework and that last for as long as the partners are committed to the union, and this gives rise to the consensual family, which contrasts with the conjugal family.

The introduction of divorce laws has allowed the rise of single-parent families (i.e., father or mother with sons/daughters) or of multi-parental families (i.e., families with sons/daughters that come from previous marriages) with the common relationship problems between parents and children. Lastly, homosexual unions are on the rise all over the world, due to their pressure for a judicial framework that is able to guarantee to them stability and social recognition.

How are we to characterize the family in the face of the various forms it takes? A Brazilian sociologist and specialist on the issue of the family, Marco Antônio Fetter, the founder of the Universidade da Família (University of the Family), a university with all levels of academic degrees, defines the family as "an ensemble of people with common objectives and with strong affective ties and bonds; and each person within this ensemble has its own defined role, where naturally the roles of the father, mother, sons/daughters and brothers/sisters emerge."[2]

A major transformation, however, took place in the family with the introduction of the condom and the pill, which have been incorporated into our culture as something normal, which makes the opposing discourse of the Catholic hierarchy outdated, and, with regards to the issue of AIDS, even cruel. It is a voice in the desert. Not even deeply committed Christians themselves listen to their discourse. The condom and the pill have set sexuality apart from procreation and from loving relationships.

Increasingly, sexuality and matrimony are seen as an opportunity for personal realization which may or may not encompass procreation. Conjugal sexuality gains in intimacy and spontaneity because through contraceptive methods and family planning it is freed from the unforeseen circumstances of an undesirable pregnancy. Sons and daughters are no longer the incidental consequence of a sexual relation; rather they are welcomed and planned in common agreement. This is a liberating experience despite the danger of individualism and despite the risk of a collapse of the family.

The emphasis on sexuality as a way for personal realization encouraged the appearance of new forms of co-habitation other than matrimony. Expressions of these new forms of co-habitation are consensual unions and partnerships (such as the co-habitation of homosexuals, men

2. See Fetter, "Família." Fetter continues and says: "There are idiosyncratic families that before would be considered absurdities: a family formed by two lesbians, one has a child by a man and the other a child by another man, and they form a very organised family—one of them functions within the phallic role and the other more like a mother . . . ; a grouping of siblings could constitute a family if one of the siblings take on the role of the father and another the role of the mother, that is to say, so that the three basic elements that normally form the family are present: the conjugal, the filial, and the fraternal. Wherever these basic roles are present I can affirm that there is a family."

and women) where the only commitment is the mutual realization of partners. Such practices, even if new, must also encompass an ethical and spiritual perspective. It is important that these practices be an expression of love and of mutual trust. A Christian reading of the phenomenon would hold that if there is love then there is something to do with God, for God is love (cf. 1 John 4:12–16). Therefore, there is no room for prejudice and discrimination. Rather, it is appropriate to respect and to be open to understand these facts and to put these facts before God. If the people involved love each other and if they take on the relation responsibly then their relationship cannot be denied a religious and spiritual relevance. Thus, an atmosphere that helps to overcome temptation and promiscuity is established and fidelity and stability are reinforced, which are at the heart of all relationships, be these through marriage or through any other form of co-habitation.

If there is sex without procreation then it is possible for procreation without sex. This is to do with the complex issue of procreation *in vitro*, of artificial insemination, and of surrogate mothers. All these issues are extremely polemical in ethical and spiritual terms and there appears to be no consensus on these issues, be this within society or be this within the churches. Generally speaking the official position of the Catholic Church is expressed, for instance, in John Paul II's encyclical *Evangelium Vitae*, which tends to a naturalistic view, and as such it demands that procreation be the result of direct sexual relations between the spouses. It demands this, when it is perfectly reasonable to accept the legitimacy of the artificial union of the wife's egg with the husband's spermatozoid and the implanting of the fertilized egg into the womb, this is all acceptable if the procedure is inspired by love and by caring for life.

To shorten my reflections on this issue, which is so complex that it is not appropriate for me to deal with here, I shall refer to the opinion of a Catholic commentator from the Netherlands on the issue:

> ... the use of technical means in connection with human procreation is far more problematical. Artificial insemination in its different forms, *in vitro* fertilization and embryo transfer, and all such technical possibilities, put us in the position on the one hand of treating sperm and ovum as "biological material" on which technical operations can be performed and into which experimental scientific investigations can be carried out (that falls outside the scope of this article), and on the other hand of achieving preg-

nancy outside the familiar framework of the traditional marriage. Thus it is possible to become pregnant by artificial insemination by donor; sperm and ovum can be brought together *in vitro* and subsequently implanted in a woman volunteer so that a child is born through a surrogate mother. Such technical possibilities are not available neutrally, in a purely instrumental capacity . . .

In reality, these methods must remain as instruments to the service of love, of help to the spouses who face problems conceiving, and always within the framework of respect for the sanctity of life.

It is not enough to procreate artificially. The human being has the right to be born humanly, of a father and a mother who, in love, desire this new life. If one has to resort to technical interventions for any problem in conceiving, then one must never lose sight of the human ambience and of the right ethical intentions.

The son/daughter that is born in these cases must be given a name, a surname, and be received into society. In these cases, the social identity is anthropologically more important than the biological identity just as in the case of Jesus in relation to Joseph. When Joseph ascribes his name to Jesus he inserts Jesus in the Davidic line and provides Jesus with a social identity. Moreover, it is important that the child be inserted into a family environment so that when the child undergoes its process of individualization it is able to overcome its Electra complex in relation to the mother and its Oedipus complex in relation to the father. In doing so the child avoids life traumas that are beyond remedy.

That said, what has to be done is to stop human procreation being handed over to technological institutions and its specialists who manipulate the "genetic material," for this would be the inauguration of the terrifying "brave new world" of H. G. Wells, which violates the sanctity of life and does away with that which is most excellent and divine in the human being: the capacity to love, and through conjugal love to pass on life, the highest development of the complexity of the universe and supreme gift of God.

THE HOLY FAMILY AND THE MODERN FAMILY

After all these issues one could certainly ask: What has the family of Nazareth to do with the modern and contradictory human family? How can the family of Nazareth illuminate and inspire us?

Before proceeding and providing an answer to these questions it is important to recognize the radical difference of situations and models of family. There is not just a temporal distance of two thousand years but also a considerable cultural distance. The family of Nazareth lived in an agrarian culture that was directly based on primary socio-economic relations. We live in a techno-scientific culture replete with gadgets that create for us a different kind of reality. Within this context the family of Nazareth cannot directly teach us anything as we inhabit completely different worlds.

But this is not all that can be said here. Within a different context the family of Nazareth has something to tell us, something that concerns us all. In those days as in our modern times, we are talking about human beings who love each other, who feel anguish, who face confusion and who search for direction, who work and who are caring. All these people live with dreams, values, and intentions of happiness and peace.

All families and all forms of co-habitation and of living together between human beings—be this between people of different genders, be this between people with the same gender, and no matter how different their life histories are—do not live off techniques or social arrangements, but off the will to find and live love and the dream to achieve fulfillment and some happiness. The unchangeable core of the family is affection, is taking care of one another, is the desire to be together, is also to be open to the procreation of new lives. This is the permanent part of a changing whole.

If this is the case then we should not primarily consider the institutional character of the family, which is the dominant perspective in ecclesiastical documents and in the reflections of theologians, we should rather consider the relational character of the family. It is important to consider the complex play of relations that takes place between partners. It is within these relations that we find life, that operate and that the utopia of love, trust, companionship and happiness functions; in short, it is within the relational character of the family that the permanent side emerges. The institutional side is made socially legitimate but it is not the origin, it is derived, it changes and it is historical. And for this reason it assumes the most different forms. Within the institutional side life is framed and rules guide relations. But these delimitations only hold their meaning when they are fed with the humus of dreams and of tender affection and through inter-communion.

Thus, what can the family of Nazareth tell us? It can precisely tell us about this side of relation, of love, of caring, of compassion, and of trust between the three of them: Jesus, Mary, and Joseph. They became Christian archetypes that, at a profound and collective level, continue to feed the imagination of the faithful and to arouse values that provide meaning and happiness to the family. These are commonly referred to as family social capital.

Trans-cultural studies reveal that the quantity and the quality of time that the members of family spend together, experiencing relations of affection and of belonging, are determining factors for individual behavior and for future social options. If the family social capital is abundant and healthy then it allows for more trust in the other and for less violence and corruption. A consequence of this is more participation in associations, in social movements, and in voluntary work. Family conflicts and the number of divorces drop dramatically. When family social capital is diluted then slowly there is the emergence of critical situations often with dramatic endings.

We could imagine that the family social capital of Jesus, Mary, and Joseph was extremely abundant. Certainly, we know little about the daily routine of the holy family. But, when I previously analyzed the historical Joseph as an artisan, husband, father, and educator, I analyzed data that yield a normal, pious, orderly, and hard-working Jewish family.

I would even dare to say that Joseph established a completely new form of co-habitation, which was even scandalous for the time: he marries a pregnant woman, and afterwards he is informed that she conceived with the help of the Holy Spirit. Joseph has the courage to take her to his home and, who knows, having to face the gossip of neighbors and the suspicions of relatives, as is implied with reason by the apocryphal writings.

One need not give in detail the values that this family had to live up to when they ran away from the bloodthirsty Herod, when they experienced the discomfort of exile, when they became bewildered when the boy demonstrated self-awareness in the Temple of Jerusalem, and lastly, when Jesus chose a pathway that was not completely understood by Mary and other relatives (cf. Mark 3:23, when they want to get hold of Jesus for they think he has lost his mind).

These values were experienced in those days and are still experienced in exactly the same way in modern times by so many families, by life partners, or by others who have chosen to live together with courage, trust, responsibility, and not rarely, within a religious and spiritual dimension.

The issue at hand is to overcome a certain moralism that is not of any help to anyone, a moralism that prejudges the various forms of the family or of co-habitation and which forces us to become unaware of the values that can be present when these forms of the family and co-habitation are lived with sincerity by people. In truth, these are the realities that matter within an ethical perspective and that are worthy in the face of God.

If the Church doctrine regarding the family has any value it is certainly the following: to remind again and again the long lasting values and to bring to the attention of Christians and other people of good will the utopian perspective of the family. Unfortunately, the Church is not always understood because the Church itself does not make it clear it is writing in a literary genre of utopia and of worldly values.

Despite this, the most frequent criticism is that, as a rule, the doctrine is abstract and unrealistic and inconsistent. If we understand the function of utopia and of the language used, as I have clarified above, then we are in a position to positively value the function of the ecclesiastical doctrine as a powerful support for family social capital.

Starting from realities that are not unknown in the papal documents, the teachings of Church seek utopian inspiration in the holy family of Jesus, Mary, and Joseph. Departing from the holy family it advances an understanding of family life that is extremely human and full of hope. In spite of all possible contradictions, this understanding can serve as the starting point for possible alternatives and new pathways alongside and along with other social enterprises that seek to rescue the family and to give it the centrality that it has for life at all stages.

This is the case, for instance, of the Apostolic Exhortation *Familiaris Consortio* and of the *Letter to Families* by John Paul II. In both documents it is emphatically stated that the family is a community of people founded in love and animated by love, whose origin and goal is the divine We.

In the *Familiaris Consortio*, the relational dimension curiously predominates the institutional dimension. The family is defined as "a complex of interpersonal relationships . . . set up—married life, fatherhood and motherhood, filiation and fraternity—through which each human person is introduced into the 'human family.'"[3]

3. John Paul II, *Familiaris Consortio*, n. 15.

These inter-personal relations turn the family into a community of people: "The family, which is founded and given by love, is a community of persons: of husband and wife, of parents and children, of relatives." Communion is that which characterizes the family: "the law of conjugal love is communion and partnership, and not domination." These are values that turn the family, as it is written in the *Catechism of the Catholic Church*, into a "sign and image of the communion of the Father and the Son in the Holy Spirit" and of the "domestic church."

What would become of the family and of partners if this utopia did not burn inside it? Is not part of love and of inter-subjective relations based on affection and care the language of dream and exaltation? Without this force that continuously animates the journey, without this niche of meaning, nobody would stand the inherent difficulties of all inter-subjective relations and the limitations of a human condition that is decadent and transitional. The family social capital would start to disappear.

These values open up the family beyond itself. The dream is to depart from the values of the family and from the different forms of the family and to give rise to the family-school, family-company, family-community, family-nation, family-humanity, and then lastly to the family-earth, which is the last step for the family-Trinity.

Therefore, the values and inspirations that gave life to the family of Nazareth continue to sustain conjugal relations, human partnerships and all those who celebrate the meaning of life in a loving and intimate relation. The God-Trinity inserted itself profoundly into the condition of a family via the trinity of Nazareth, even to the point of personifying itself, and continues to aid human beings in their searching. The forms and the ways may vary, however, the love and the communion that direct human hearts towards one another and in the direction of the great Other that is the Trinity of Persons, eternally exchanging life, love, and communion, do not change.

12

The Figure of the Father in Light of Saint Joseph

The situation of fatherhood is even more problematic than the situation of the modern family. We live in a society that is either fatherless or in which the figure of the father is absent. In a sense, the figure of the father has been expelled from the family to the measure in which he was stopped fulfilling his paternal functions. Be this the outcome of the work regime in industrial and techno-scientific societies, which occupies the father mentally and physically in such an extreme way that he has very little time to spend with his children; or be this because his role has been eroded by criticisms of the authority of the father, which is identified as patriarchalism or equated with machismo, which are objects of fierce challenges by the various feminist movements. Men, in general, and fathers, in particular, have faced a strong identity crisis and they have not emerged from this crisis yet.

THE ECLIPSE OF THE FIGURE OF THE FATHER

It has already been said that modern man succumbed to the "syndrome of God." Men, since the Neolithic period and with the rise of patriarchalism, took on a number of tasks, and did not share these tasks with women. Men started to be heads of the family, to organize public life, create and organize the state, assemble together mechanisms of power, and make wars. To all these tasks, men associated the ideology of power, efficiency, and victory. Man can never fail and man can never lose because man is a little god on Earth.

As it happens, modern society has reached a level of complexity that is beyond the human capacity of management and control. Man has increasingly become a god of mockery. He can fail and has failed; he is not a god but a frail, simple mortal, who cries and screams for help. But society continues to demand from him, and he does not know how to cope with these requests. Hence the eclipse of the traditional figure of the father.

Even the simple image of the hardworking father is being eroded; his profession becomes increasingly hidden from his children; the social division of labor, the distance between home and work place, the status of wage earner, the oppressing influence of the media over social and family habits, all this has destroyed the aura of the paternal authority. The father is downgraded to the level of a connecting link without great relevance in the complex machinery of society. The anti-patriarchal critique has developed into an anti-father critique and the result of this is a considerable loss to the family and to the children.

Social order is no longer based in a particular subject—the symbolic and archetypal figure of the father, which guaranteed stability, conferred security and provided a sense of direction—but in a hierarchy of employees who officially fulfill their functions. Once their duties are fulfilled they return to the egalitarian world of kinsman.

A well-known commentator on the sociology of fatherhood asserts that: "Patriarchal society has been replaced by the fatherless society or by a fraternal society that performs anonymous tasks and that is ruled by impersonal forces." Such a claim does not represent an anomaly per se but a particular phenomenon of modern societies.

The importance of the Protestant Reformation is well known, with its ascetic morality, for the makeup of the modern world, which is founded on productive work and the accumulation of wealth. It is worth noting here that a particular aspect of the Reformation has impinged strongly upon the family.[1] Up to the time of the Reformation, marriage was understood as a sacrament, therefore as something that bears a connection to the sacred, to God and with God's blessing. The father was understood, in a certain way, as a reflection of the celestial Father, and as such, he was surrounded by respect and authority. Luther, who did not find proof in the Bible that could justify marriage as a sacrament, negated this, and in so doing removed from marriage its sacred aspect. He considered marriage to be a merely secular reality (*weltliches Ding*). The father was then relinquished to producing. He does not affirm his authority with reference to the celestial father any longer, he rather affirms his authority with reference to his performance in his effort to produce goods and

---

1. See the appropriate reflections on this issue in Risé, *Il Padre*.

of providing for his family. Hence, a complete symbolic framework that conferred dignity and centrality to the father was destroyed. Instead of the paternal archetype with all the resonances that it has for human interiority, we have in force the paternal function of the provider.

THE SOCIETY OF THE GREAT MOTHER
AND THE CRISES OF THE FATHER

That which replaced the patriarchal society was the society of the Great Mother, and this is the kind of society that is in force today. It was organized (especially the welfare state) in such a way that it fulfills the functions of the mother: it satisfies the needs of its citizens, it provides healthcare, education, social security, it maintains the status quo, it eliminates risks, everything is under control so that the wheels of society always run smoothly.

This kind of situation has placed a challenge to the identity of the father, who used to fulfill the function of Great providing Father. The father now sees himself misplaced and, when he finds himself unemployed (and there are millions of unemployed in any given country) he feels demoralized and even abused.

The weakening of the figure of the father has destabilized the family. The rise in divorce rates is so high that we see the rise of a society of broken families and of divorced people in their on right. The proportion of divorces in the United States, for instance, is astonishing: one in two, with the tendency to reach two in three, marriages ending up in divorce. According to current legislation in force in the United States, but also in Europe, the children of these marriages are judicially placed in the sole custody of the mother, who often cuts all ties with the father. Here arises, without a doubt, not only the eclipse of the father but also the social death of the father.

The consequences for the children are dramatic. Recent official statistics from the United States show a sorrowful picture: 90 percent of the children who run away or who are homeless come from families without a father; 70 percent of young offenders come from families where the father was absent; 85 percent of youngsters in prison grew up in families without a father; 63 percent of youngsters who commit suicide had absent fathers. Such a scenario demonstrates a human and social disaster.[2]

2. These figures are given by Risé in "Alla Ricerca del'Padre." See also from this same

The absence of the father is, by all means, unacceptable. It removes a structuring factor from the children, it takes away a direction in life, it debilitates the will to take on a project, and it mutilates society as if an important organ, such as an eye, an arm or a leg, had been severed.

The current situation of the father does not serve as a basis for an experience of God as Father. Psychoanalytic tradition has maintained the importance of the father figure and of the experiences that the children have with him so that they are able to project an image of an integrating and humanizing God-Father—i.e., an Oedipus well-realized.[3] In order for the father to continue to perform this transcendental function and true mission it is imperative to re-organize, with different foundations, the figure of the father. It is with this in mind that the figure of Saint Joseph, as a father, can be of help.

THE ANTHROPOLOGICAL PRINCIPLE OF THE FATHER AND HISTORICAL MODELS

Before continuing it is of extreme importance to make a distinction between models of fatherhood and the anthropological principle of the father. This distinction, which is neglected in many fields and even in the sciences, will help us to avoid misunderstandings and recover the permanent and inalienable value of the figure of the father.

Psychoanalytic tradition, be it with reference to Freud or to Jung, demonstrated the extreme importance of the anthropological principle of the mother and, in connection with this, of the anthropological principle of the father in the constitution and development of the human being. The anthropological principle of the father is our particular concern here.

The father is responsible for the first and necessary rupture in the intimate relation between the mother and her child, and he is also responsible for the introduction of the child to another sphere, the transpersonal sphere, the sphere of the father, of siblings, of grandparents, of relatives, and of others in society.

---

author (a Jungian psychoanalyst, a professor at Trieste, and an expert on "fatherhood"): "L'Occidente senza Padre."

3. The most important texts on this issue have been put together by Mendel in *La Révolte contre le Pere.*

Within the transpersonal and social sphere, which is represented by the figure of the father, is order, discipline, rights, duties, authority, and the limits that must be respected between one group and another. Within this sphere, people work, fulfill projects, seek directions for life projects, innovate, and improvise. For this reason, they must show confidence, courage, and the willingness to make sacrifices, be this in order to overcome difficulties or be this in order to achieve objectives.

Well, the father is the archetype and the symbolic personification of all these attitudes. He is the gateway to the trans-personal and social world. When the child enters this sphere it must get its bearings through someone. This someone is the father, who appears as a hero, as the one who knows everything, who is allowed to do everything, and who does everything. If the child lacks this reference the child feels insecure, lost, and without the capacity to take initiative.

It is at this moment that a process of fundamental importance for the child's psyche takes place, a process which bears consequences for the child's entire life: the recognition of authority and the acceptance of limits that are acquired through the figure of the father.

The child comes from an experience based on the mother, based on a cozy relationship, on the satisfaction of its desires, on the warmth of the intimacy where everything is safe, in a kind on non-duality. From this set up, the child must learn something new: that this new trans-personal and social sphere is not an extension of the mother and that there are conflicts and limits within it. It is the father who leads the child in the discovery of this new dimension. The father appears with his life history and example as a bearer of authority, capable of imposing limits and establishing duties with his own authority.

It is particular to the father to teach the child the meaning of these limits and the value of authority, without which one enters into society with some traumas. In this phase, the child releases itself from the mother, even to the extent that it does not wish to obey the mother as much, and gets closer to the father. The child demands to be loved by the father and awaits clarifications from him for all new problems that it faces. It is the task of the father to explain to the child that it must continue to obey the mother because, as his wife, she is entrusted by him in his absence to impose the limits and the discipline he implemented. By speaking in this manner to the child, the child recovers its harmonic relationship with the mother, respects the mother's authority—without, however, being blindly submissive to her as happened in the previous maternal phase.

It is the father's responsibility to make the child understand that life is not only enjoyment, but also work, life is not only goodness, but also conflict, life is not only success, but also failure, and that life is not solely about gaining, but also loosing. If the mother has the tendency to fulfill the child's desires, if entertainment programs on television only exacerbate desires by portraying that the sky is the limit, then it is the father's responsibility to demonstrate that everything has a limit and suitability, that we are all beings of incompleteness, limitations, and mortality, even if the child starts to consider him boring and insupportable. To operate this truly uncomfortable pedagogy, but which is vital, is to listen to the call of the anthropological principle of the father. If he does not take on this symbolic and archetypal function, the empiric and concrete father is greatly jeopardizing his child, perhaps even in a long-lasting way.

A society that systematically criticizes a model of fatherhood, the patriarchal model—and by doing this damages with its unqualified criticisms the anthropological principle of fatherhood—is a society that starts to loose its bearings, it is a society that experiences the growth of violence, that witnesses the erosion of authority and that allows for the lack of limits in social relations. This kind of society is either close to chaos or condemned to the return of the father, but who returns this time in the corrupt form of authoritarianism, of dictatorship, and of the terrorism of the state.

What happens when the father is absent from the family or when the family is only established around the mother? The children become somehow mutilated because they show themselves to be insecure and incapable of defining life projects. They show great difficulty in accepting the principle of authority and the existence of limits. Something is not working properly in their inner being. They live in a permanent conflict between the archetypal father, who is the gateway to the social world and whom they feel absent and even miss, and the concrete mother, whom they live with and who represents the home, coziness, and intimacy but which is insufficient to provide sustainability in the process of self-individuation.

From the non-resolution of this conflict results a weakening of the masculine in the children, causing the children to lack the necessary energies to build up their identity, to define a life pathway and innovate and improvise. In time, the most dramatic effect of this situation has already been pointed out previously: the high rates of anti-social and devious behavior.

Hence, on the one hand is this anthropological principle of fatherhood, a permanent structure that is fundamental to the process of individualization of each human being. This personalizing function is not condemned to disappear. It continues and will continue to be internalized by children as a matrix in the proper formation of character. The children crave it. On the other hand are the historical and social models that have embodied the anthropological principle of fatherhood. These are ever changing and diverse in history and in different cultures. These models pass us by.

For instance, one example is the way in which the figure of the father appears in some Arabic cultures, with many wives, with absolute authority and master of the family. Another is the patriarchal father of the traditional countryside culture, with strong traces of machismo. Another is the father of an urban and bourgeoisie culture, a father that is invisible and dispensable, victim of the crisis faced by his culture, as I have argued previously.

Models are always different. But the anthropological principle of fatherhood acts in all of these models without, however, being exhausted in any of them. In some of these models it finds more space for a humanizing realization, in others it gains pathological forms, and in all of them it shares the human condition, which is marked by contradictions, advances and withdrawals, realizations and frustrations.

It is also important to recognize that everywhere we see concrete examples of fatherhood emerging that are immune to patriarchal strains and who live with dignity in the new globalized society that is rising. They work, fulfill their duties, show themselves to be responsible and determined people, and in this way they fulfill their archetypal and symbolic function for their children—a function which is indispensable for the child's *I* to mature without confusions and traumas and ingress into autonomous life until it reaches the moment when it becomes a mother or father itself.

SAINT JOSEPH—AN EXAMPLE OF FATHERHOOD

Telemachus, son of Odysseus in Homer's *Odyssey*, said the following words that are still relevant today: "If what mortals most desire could be achieved in the blink of an eye, the first thing I would want would be the return of my father" (*Odyssey* 16.147–49). Here is the anguish, ancient and modern, of the son without a father. This anguish permeates all areas of our culture. Thus, I ask: In what sense can the figure of Saint Joseph help us? It is appropriate to remind the reader that Saint Joseph, beyond being the historical father figure for Jesus and husband of Mary, has become a powerful archetype in his own right. As an archetype, he embodies a collective character and radiates in the psyche of Christians, for whom the figure of Saint Joseph has great existential meaning.

I am not concerned here with comparing models of fatherhood, namely that of Saint Joseph and the modern model. These are so distant from each other that, practically, there are no points in common between them. Rather, what I am interested in is that the attitudes, values, and virtues lived by Saint Joseph have attained an archetypal function for modern fathers. These attitudes, values, and virtues are part of being human and they can inspire us. They reveal a father in the plenitude of fatherhood. They do not reveal Saint Joseph through words since he did not leave us anything written; rather, they reveal Saint Joseph through his example, which is more powerful than words.

As a man, groom, and husband of Mary, he radiated the anthropological principle of fatherhood. This is shown at various moments in his history. Firstly, he showed an important virtue of any father: the determination to make a decision when faced with a complex problem (such as the mysterious pregnancy of Mary) and innovating and improvising (such as when he takes Mary to his house).

As a father, he showed a strong sense of duty: he went with Mary to Bethlehem because of the Roman census, stayed beside her when she was in labor in the grotto in Bethlehem and took all the care that the situation demanded. Afterwards, alongside Mary he fulfilled his religious duty of going to the Temple in Jerusalem to purify, to present the boy and to attend the yearly festival in Jerusalem at the time of Passover.

As a father, he showed courage by facing up to the risk of the deadly persecution by Herod, by facing up to the anguish and austerity of a hasty escape to exile in Egypt, and by taking the decision to return and hide the family in Nazareth in the north of the country.

As a father, he exercised authority and imposed limits; this is something that became apparent when Jesus was left behind at the Temple. When he did not find Jesus in the caravan, father and mother returned worried to Jerusalem and reprimanded their son: "Son why have you treated us so?" (Luke 2:48). They imposed limits on Jesus because the Scriptures are clear that Jesus "was obedient to them" (Luke 2:51). To obey is to embrace the authority of the father and to accept the limits that have been imposed. The Letter to the Hebrews later reminds us that Jesus, "Although he was a Son, he learned obedience through what he suffered" (Heb 5:8). In the apocryphal writings, as we have seen, Joseph reprimands Jesus many times and even pulls his ears. That is to say, he exercised his paternal authority and knew how to impose limits on his naughty son.

It is a function of the father to be the bridge between the family and society. For Semitic cultures the ritual of naming the child by the father was a way for the father to assume publicly the paternity of the child and for this to be recognized by the extended family and society. Joseph assumes this function even knowing that he could not be the biological father of Jesus. He performs the ritual of naming the child and within the Semitic understanding becomes father (cf. Matt 1:21). Jesus can publicly call Joseph father, as the gospels confirm.

It is also part of the function of being a social gateway to pass on to the child some professional experience. Jesus becomes an artisan and carpenter and as such he was publicly known at the time (cf. Matt 13:54–56; Luke 4:25; John 1:45; 6:42).

Lastly, the healthy and vigorous paternity of Joseph served as a basis for Jesus' spiritual experience as he calls God 'abba. If Jesus showed extreme intimacy with God in his public life by calling him by the infantile term "Daddy" ('abba), this means that he lived a similar experience of extreme intimacy with his father Joseph.

Joseph's behavior as a father, when analyzed through the categories available in our culture, allow for presenting Saint Joseph as an exemplary figure without pious and moralistic appeals. Saint Joseph is an exemplary figure whom we can connect with and from whom we can learn important lessons. This is especially the case for fathers in the twenty-first century, who live in a model of civilization that is extremely different and who are in search of a kind of identity that is appropriate for our times.

Saint Joseph helps us rescue fatherhood. His example of fatherhood can enrich a father's identity and provide some impetus while facing the challenges of modern society, especially the challenges of this globalized age of humanity.

Conclusion: The Entire Holy Trinity Is among Us

By speaking about Saint Joseph I have also spoken about God and about God within the Christian understanding, which is always as a Trinity: Father, Son, and Holy Spirit. I understand that this is the most appropriate way of speaking about Saint Joseph, that is, by making reference to that which is principal, the Trinity of God.

A COMPLETE AND ENCOMPASSING UNDERSTANDING OF GOD

The Christian understanding about Saint Joseph has slowly matured throughout the centuries. And it has matured so much that in our modern times Saint Joseph is perceived as belonging to the hypostatic order, that is, Saint Joseph takes part in the triune God's self-communication to humanity.

This is without doubt true, for the Magisterium of the Church itself officially defends this view, as is demonstrated by the Apostolic Exhortation of Pope John Paul II about Saint Joseph, the *Redemptoris Custos*. There it is clearly said that the mystery of the incarnation of God not only assumed reality in Jesus, but "was also 'taken up' in Joseph's human fatherhood."[1] Theology had previously established Saint Joseph's relation with the Word, for he is the father of Jesus, and theology had also established Saint Joseph's relation with the Holy Spirit, for he is Mary's husband. Saint Joseph's relation with the celestial Father was missing, for Saint Joseph is also a father. It is to the merit of the theology developed in the second half of the twentieth century to pursue a theological understanding in this direction, and it is an achievement when it was explicitly said by a Brazilian of the Amazon region, Brother Adauto Schumaker:

1. John Paul II, *Redomptoris Custos*, n. 21.

156

Saint Joseph is the personification of the Father. My efforts in this book were to provide a solid theological basis for this understanding. And we have finally reached the point in which we have been awarded a complete and encompassing understanding of the divine reality and of the human reality. The Trinity, which is the Divine Family in the heavens, personified itself in the human family on earth. The Father personified himself in Joseph, the Son personified himself in Jesus, and the Holy Spirit personified itself in Mary. Each human family and each human being were inserted into this personification because we are all, consciously or not, brothers and sisters of Jesus, Mary, and Joseph. The same humanity that is in them and that was assumed by the Holy Trinity is also in us. Therefore, something of our shared humanity belongs permanently to the triune God. The infinite desire that consumes us finds its everlasting satisfaction here.

DAILY SPIRITUALITY

Good theology must end up in spirituality. Hence, I wish to emphasize here some issues regarding the kind of spirituality that is derived from the silence and from the anonymous life of an artisan-carpenter of Nazareth. The fact that he belongs to the hypostatic order neither nullifies nor modifies the normal human order of things.

The same affirmations of the Council of Chalcedon (451 CE) concerning the incarnation of the Word in Jesus are also valid with regards to Saint Joseph, the personification of the Father. There it is stated that Jesus is simultaneously God and man, without confusion, without mutation, without division, and without the separation of the human and divine essences. The properties of each essence are preserved. This means that everything that is human is present in Jesus: happiness and anguish, love and indignation, intimacy with God and temptations. But because of the union of the essences in the same Person these properties become inter-changeable, that is, the properties of God become the properties of the man, and the properties of the man become properties of God. It follows from this that God was born, God got annoyed, God cried and God died. It also follows that the man is infinite and that the man is eternal. And by applying this same dialectical understanding to Saint Joseph we reach the following: Saint Joseph lived just like any other carpenter of his time; he was pious and well-integrated in the community (the common understanding of "just"); he was a loyal husband and a careful father; he experienced crises and anguish (cf. Matt 1:19–20), fears and concerns which are something normal to those who flee from mortal persecution with wife and son; and he also experienced other situations of happiness and realization which are inherent to the human condition.[2] But because Saint Joseph was the personification of the Father, all those realities experienced by him also belong to the Father.

SAINT JOSEPH, PATRON OF THE "DOMESTIC CHURCH"

From the Father's perspective, all personification means also a *kenosis*, that is, a lowering, a renunciation of the Father's divine attributes, and it also means an insertion into the ambiguity of the human realm. The invisible Father turned himself invisible in Joseph. The Father of the eternal silence turned himself into temporal silence within the life of Joseph.

This *kenosis* has great theological significance, and it is the foundation of a kind of spirituality that has been greatly forgotten by official Christianity. Within official Christianity the popes, the bishops, the priests, the preachers and the ministers occupy the central stage as they speak, teach, encourage, and direct the community of faith. It is the official Christianity that is visible.

But alongside this official Christianity there is also the popular, the daily, the anonymous Christianity, which is not visible, which is not shown in the media, and which is not very much noticed by the institutional Church itself. The great majority of Christians, our grandparents, our parents, and our uncles and aunts, live within this popular Christianity; they take the gospel seriously and they feel inspired by the practices of Jesus and of the apostles. Saint Joseph, for his silence and anonymity, is also founded within popular Christianity. More than patron of the universal Church, as desired by the popes, Saint Joseph is the true patron of the "domestic Church, the church of the little brothers and sisters of Jesus (cf. Matt 25:40).

Without a doubt, the great majority of the faithful live in anonymity, buried in their grey daily lives, earning their living with hard work, supporting their families as best they can, and cheering themselves up or suffering on the weekends due to their victories or defeats depending on how they feel. By and large they are honorable, giving, and religious. But

2. See the well-argued paper by Siuta, "Saint Joseph et les Crises de la Vie."

they are of a popular religiosity, they are more guided by the feeling of God than by the doctrines about God. For the great majority of people God and his presence in various circumstances of life are existential certainties. God is not a problem, rather God is the light for all problems.

THE SPIRITUALITY OF THE "GOOD PEOPLE"

The "good people" live the spirituality of the *poor of Yahweh* as the Judeo-Christian Scriptures would call them.[3] Poverty here has more to do with a fundamental attitude of being open to and welcoming God than with a social condition of material poverty. Certainly, material poverty facilitates living with this attitude of openness because normally people in need beg God for help with their tribulations. But this attitude is not conditioned to material poverty, for among the poor of Yahweh are also found people belonging to better off social classes. People from these better off social classes can also be open to God, which is something that is demonstrated through their openness towards the poor.

Saint Joseph is found among these poor of Yahweh.[4] How are we to translate this biblical expression into something more modern and more easily understandable to people who do not possess religious references? I would say that the poor of Yahweh are those that are commonly called "good people."

Who are these "good people"? It is not easy to provide a characterization for this concept. However, we encounter "good people" at every moment of our lives. The "good people" are the people who are honest, just, and hardworking, are the people in well-integrated families, are the people who are always willing to help others and who show their integrity every day. If it is difficult to characterize the concept "good people," it is not, however, difficult to identify "good people." For "good people" are welcoming, are not malicious looking, have an open face, and irradiate an aura of goodness. We feel well when we are close to "good people." We feel we can trust in "good people." Just as the poor of Yahweh are

3. There is a vast exegetical literature on this issue, which has been produced mainly by commentators connected with Liberation Theology; cf. Gutiérrez, *A Theology of Liberation* and *The Power of the Poor in History*; Pixley and Clodovis Boff, *Opção pelos pobres*; George, " Pauvre"; Gelin, *Les Pauvres que Dieu Aime*.

4. See the excellent essay by Robert, "Joseph de Bethléem et la Spiritualité des Pauvres de Yahvé."

not to be only found amongst the materially poor, so it is with "good people," who can also be found amongst the more well-to-do strata in society. These are peoples who keep, in spite of difficulties, their essential humanity immune to the deceptions of the society of representation—a society greatly concerned with image rather than content. For this reason "good people" is more to do with a state of spirit than with belonging to a social class, it is more to do with a property of the heart that is present in all social classes than a privilege inherent to a particular social class. "Good people" are those who in the work place are happy to replace the workmate who has not turned up because this is the way things should be and because things need to continue functioning, and it does not matter if sacrifices need to be made. Or for instance, the cook who stays after her working hours without complaining because of a family function that is going on for longer than expected. Or the restaurant owner who is concerned with ecological issues in his or her community and who is not concerned with loosing a few costumers and some money so that he or she can coordinate workshops, always be present, and encourage participation in community activities. "Good people" do not need to be religious, but they are always respectful, and when they are religious they do not need to show off; they discreetly say their prayers and they always trust in the good God. "Good people" are similar to the "humble people" of the wonderful song by Chico Buarque,[5] they are those who live in the suburbs and who, late afternoon, sit on their verandas to talk and to see life passing by, they are those who face up to life alone with no help from anyone. And they are courageous, honest, and hardworking.

Saint Joseph is the representative of "good people" and of "humble people." He is amongst the crowds of the "good people" of humankind. These crowds make things move forward and allow societies to function in spite of corrupt politicians, who in general lie about the real situation regarding poverty in the country and around the world.

Norberto Bobbio (1909–2004), the great Italian philosopher on politics and modern democracy, left us a wise lesson: the value of a society is not to be measured through the legal apparatus that it flouts, but by the virtues that its citizens live and experience. The "good people" live

5. Translator's note: Francisco Buarque de Hollanda, best known as Chico Buarque, is a Brazilian singer, composer, dramatist, and writer. The song "Gente Humilde" (Humble People) was written in 1969.

simply and virtuously, they are those who honor their people and who build their country.

Saint Joseph is adorned with these simple and anonymous virtues as I have tried to demonstrate in various passages of this book. It is my understanding that the highest praise to Jesus found in the gospels is not that he is the awaited Messiah, the Son of Man, and Son of God. All these statements are true and important for our understanding of the real identity of Jesus. The highest and most acceptable praise, however, is when they testify: "He has done all things well; he even makes the deaf hear and the dumb speak" (Mark 7:37).

We can say the same about Saint Joseph: he did everything well. He was simply "a just man" as the Gospel of Saint Matthew says (cf. Matt 1:19), and this concept encompasses human and divine virtues.

My theological efforts were to unveil the dimensions of mystery that enveloped the figure of Saint Joseph and demonstrate that Saint Joseph is the personification of the celestial Father, without diminishing in any way whatsoever his "being just" and the anonymity of his life and deeds. These are everlasting values for Christians, especially for those who live in the same kind of humble condition that Saint Joseph lived, and this is beyond any theological reflection.

Saint Joseph possibly did not understand anything about theology, nor about the scribes, nor about the Pharisees of his time, nor about the churches of our modern times, and even less about the theological argument I have tried to elaborate in this book. This does not matter. It was more important for Joseph to live firmly grounded in sincerity and humility, which are the virtues of the father, the husband, the educator, and of the worker, than to understand himself as the personification of the Father. In these virtues and through these virtues the celestial Father showed himself as subtle signs.

I conclude this book with the words of an apocryphal writing that inspired my research and which I wish to be a call to all Christians, men and women: "And you have ordered us to go into all the world and preach the Holy Gospel; and you have said: Relate to them the death of my father Joseph, and celebrate to him with annual solemnity a festival and a sacred day" (*History of Joseph the Carpenter* 30). I did my part. It is now left to others to complete any issue left unanswered by me and to expand our knowledge about the mystery of God's personification in the humble figure of Saint Joseph.

Prayer to Saint Joseph

Dear Saint Joseph,
You were a worker as we are and you know tiredness and sweat,
    help us guarantee work for all.

You were a just man who conducted, in your workplace and in the community,
    a life of integrity at the service of God and others.
Make us also good in our works
    and aware of the needs of others.

You were the husband who took Mary already pregnant
    by the Holy Spirit to your home.
Make our parents welcome the lives that God sends them.

You accepted to be the father of Jesus and you took care of him against those
    who wanted to kill him, and you protected him during your escape to Egypt.
Make our parents protect their sons and daughters against addictive drugs
    and against serious illnesses.

You were Jesus' educator, teaching him to read the Scriptures
    and introducing him to the traditions of your people.
Make us continue our family piety and always remember God
    in everything we do.

Dear Saint Joseph,
In your human face we see portrayed the face of the divine Father.
May He welcome us, protect us, and provide us with the assurance
    that we walk in the palm of his hand.

Show us, Saint Joseph, the power of your fatherhood:
> Give us determination in the face of problems,
> courage in the face of peril,
> awareness of the limits of our powers,
> and infinite trust in the celestial Father.

We ask all these in the power of the Father,
> in the love of the Son,
> and in the zeal of the Holy Spirit.

Amen.

Bibliography

Almendariz, L. M. "El Padre maternal." *Estudios Eclesiásticos* 58 (1983) 249–75.

Algermissen, Konrad. *Lexikon der Marienkunde*. Regensburg: Pustet, 1967.

Ante-Nicene Christian Library: Translations of The Writings of the Fathers. Elibron Classics, 2005.

Argentan, Louis-François d'. *Conférences theologique et spirituelles sur les Grandeurs de la tres-Vierge Marie, Mere de Dieu*. Rouen: Vaultier, 1680.

Aron, Robert. *Gli anni oscuri di Gesù*. Milano: Mondadori, 1978.

Augustine, *De Trinitate*.

Bach, José Marcos. *O Futuro da Família: Tendências e Perspectivas*. Petrópolis: Vozes, 1983.

———. *Evolução do Amor Conjugal*. Petrópolis: Vozes, 1980.

Bauer, Walter. *Griechisch-deutsches Wörterbuch zum Neuen Testament*. 5th ed. Berlin: Töpelmann, 1958.

Bellovet, L. "Le Pére de la Miséricorde, Saint Joseph appartient-il à l'Ordre Hypostatique?" *La Science Catholique* 8 (1894) 490–510.

Bertolin, José Antonio. "San Giuseppe nel Brasile durante il XVIII secolo." *Estudios Josefinos* 45 (1991) 687–703.

Bertrand, Guy-M. *Dictionnaire de Spiritualité*. Paris: Beauchesne, 1975; see "Joseph," col. 1301–2.

Bérulle, Pierre de. *Oeuvres Completes*. Introduction and notes by Michel Depuy. Vol. 3.1: *Discours de l'état et des grandeurs de Jésus*. Paris: Cerf, 1995–2006.

Blinzer, Josef. *Die Brüder und Schwestern Jesu*. Stuttgarter Bibelstudien 21. Stuttgart: Katholisches Bibelwerk, 1969.

Boff, Clodovis. *O Cotidiano de Maria de Nazaré*. São Paulo: Salesiana, 2003.

Boff, Leonardo. *Ave Maria: O Feminino e o Espírito Santo*. Petrópolis: Vozes, 1980.

———. *Cry of the Earth, Cry of the Poor*. Maryknoll, NY: Orbis, 1997.

———. *O Evangelho do Cristo Cósmico*. Petrópolis: Vozes, 1971.

———. *Jesus Christ Liberator: A Critical Christology for Our Times*. Translated by Patrick Hughes. Maryknoll, NY: Orbis, 1978.

———. *The Maternal Face of God: The Feminine and Its Religious Expressions*. Translated by Robert R. Barr and John W. Dierksmeier. San Francisco: Harper & Row, 1989.

————. *O Pai-Nosso: A Oração da Libertação Integral.* Petrópolis: Vozes, 2003.

————. *A Ressureição de Cristo e a Nossa Na Morte.* Petrópolis: Vozes, 2003.

————. "O sacramento do matrimônio: símbolo do amor de Deus para com os homens do mundo presente." In *O Destino do Homen e do Mundo,* 137–56. Petrópolis: Vozes, 2002.

————. *A Santíssima Trindade é a Melhor Comunidade.* Petrópolis: Vozes, 2003.

————. *Trinity and Society.* Translated by Paul Burns. Theology and Liberation Series. Maryknoll, NY: Orbis, 1988.

————, and R. M. Murraro. *Masculino e Feminino: Uma Nova Consciência para of Encontro das Differenças.* Rio de Janeiro: Sextante, 2002.

Bossuet, Jacques Bénigne. *Oeuvres de Bossuet.* Vol. 3: *Sermons, Panégyriques, Méditations sur l'évangile.* Paris: Didot, 1847.

Bourassa Perrota, L. *Saint Joseph: His Life and His Role in the Church Today.* Huntington, IN: Our Sunday Visitor Publishing, 2000.

Bouyer, L. *Le Père Invisible: Approches du Mystère de la divinité.* Paris: Cerf, 1976.

Brändle, F. "Jesús Nazareno por que? El Puesto de José en el Camino de la Revelación." *Cahiers de Joséphologie* 39 (1991) 34–41.

Brown, Raymond E. "L'Annonce à Joseph (Mt 1, 18–25)." In *La Figure de Joseph à l'orée du troisième millénaire.* Cahiers de l'Oratoire Saint Joseph 6. Montreal: Centre de Recherce et de Documentation, Oratoire Saint-Joseph, 1999.

Carrasco, J. A. "Influencia negativa de los apócrifos en la josefología." *Estudios Josefinos* 47 (1993) 29–45.

————. "Ritual del matrimonio de Maria y José." *Estudios Josefinos* 51 (1997) 25–39.

Carthagena, J. *Homilia catholicae de sacris arcanis Deiparae Mariae et St Josephi eiusdem sponsi.* Neapoli: Vernieri, 1859.

Charbonneau, Paul-Eugène. "L'appartenance de Saint Joseph à l'ordre de l'union hypostatique et son rôle de patron de l'Eglise Universelle." *Cahiers de Joséphologie* 3 (1955) 241–74.

————. *Saint-Joseph appartient-il à l'ordre de l'union hypostatique?* Montreal: Centre de Recherche Oratoire de Saint-Joseph e Faculté de Théologie, 1961.

Charmot, Francois. *La Sainte Trinité et S. Joseph.* Rome: Pisani, 1960.

Châtelier, Louis. *L'Europe des dévôts XVI–XVIII siècle.* Paris: Flammarion, 1987.

————. *The Europe of the Devout: The Catholic Reformation and the Formation of a New Society.* Translated by Jean Birrell. Past and Present Publications. Cambridge: Cambridge University Press, 1989.

Chouraqui, André. *La Vie Quotidienne des Hommes de la Bible.* Paris: Hachette, 1978.

Claudel, Paul. "Letter Published in Paris, 1934." In *Positions et propositions,* 2:147–49. Paris: Gallimard, 1948.

Clavel, Bernard. *Jésus, le Fils du Charpentier.* Paris: Laffont, 1996.

————. *Joseph, Fils de David, Qui êtes-vous?* Burtin: Lion de Juda, 1987.

CNBB. *Casamento e família no mundo de hoje: textos seletos do magistério eclesial.* Petrópolis: Vozes, 1994.

Couture, Maurice. *Saint Joseph Époux et Père: Un Modèle pour Tous.* Montreal: Carmel, 1997.

Daniel-Rops, Henri. *Daily Life in Palestine at the Time of Christ.* London: Phoenix, 2002.

———. *A Vida Diária no Tempo de Jesus.* São Paulo: Vida Nova, 1983.

Davies, H., *Christian Worship: Its History and Meaning,* New York: Abingdon, 1957.

Deiss, Lucien. *Joseph, Marie et Jésus.* Versailles: Saint Paul, 1997.

De La Noi, P. *De la Redemptoris Custos a la teología dogmática,* 171–75. Centre de Documentación y Estudios Josefinos de Mexico, 2001.

Denzinger, Heinrich, and Adolf Schönmelzer. *Enchiridion Symbolorum.* New York: Crossroads, 1998.

Devasahayam, S. J., *Saint Joseph for the Third Millenium.* Mumbai: Pauline Publications, 1999.

Dobraczynski, J. *L'ombra del Padre: il romanzo di Giuseppe.* Brescia: Morcelliana, 1982.

Dolto, Françoise, and Gérard Séverin. *L'évangile au risque de la psychanalyse.* Paris: Delarge, 1977.

———. "O Complexo de Édipo, Suas Etapas Estruturantes e Seus Acidentes." In *No jogo do desejo.* São Paulo, Ática, 1981.

Doze, Andrew. *Joseph, Ombre du Père.* Nouan-le-Fuselier: Lion de Juda, 1989.

———. "Marie rélève Joseph." *Cahiers de L'Oratoire Saint-Joseph* 11 (2001) 33–59.

———. *Saint Joseph: Shadow of the Father.* Translated by Florestine Audett. New York: Alba, 1992.

Dubois, Louis Ernest, Cardinal. *Saint Joseph.* 7th ed. Paris: Gabalda, 1927.

Dulles, Avery. *Revelation Theology.* New York: Herder, 1969.

Durrwell, F. X. *Le Père: Dieu et son Mystère.* Théologies. Paris: Cerf, 1993.

Edinger, Edward F. *The Bible and the Psyche: Individuation Symbolism in the Old Testament.* Studies in Jungian Psychology by Jungian Analysts 24. Toronto: Inner City, 1986.

Elliott, J. K., editor. *Apocryphal New Testament: A Collection of Apocryphal Christian Literature in an English Translation.* Oxford: Oxford University Press, 1994.

Enciclopedia Cattolica, 8:805–55. Vatican City, 1951.

Ephraïm, Joseph. *Joseph, un Père pour le Nouveau Millénaire.* Nouan-le-Fuselier: Béatitudes, 1996.

Erbetta, Mario. *Gli apocrifi del Nuovo Testamento.* Torino: Marietti,1975.

Ferraro, B., *Cristologia.* Petrópolis: Vozes, 2004.

Fetter, Marco Antônio. "Família: os desafios de uma instituição em crise." *Correio Riograndense* 29 (October 2003) 11.

Filas, Francis Lad. *Joseph and Jesus: A Theological Study of Their Relationship.* Milwaukee: Bruce, 1952.

———. *The Man Nearest to Christ: Nature and Historic Development of the Devotion to St. Joseph.* Milwaukee: Bruce, 1946.

———. *Saint Joseph après le Concile Vatican II.* Montreal: Fides, 1970.

Foucher, Daniel. *Notre Père, Joseph le Charpentier.* La Chapelle de Montligeon: Montligeon, 1999.

Freud, Sigmund. *The Interpretation of Dreams.* Oxford: Oxford University Press, 1999.

Gächter, P. "Die Brüder Jesu." *Zeitschrift für katholische Theologie* 89 (1967) 458–69.

Gallbach, M. R. *Learning from Dreams*. Einsiedeln, Switzerland: Daimon, 2006.

Galot, P. "Pour une Théologie du Père." *Esprit et Vie* 94 (1984) 497–503; 661–69; 95 (1985) 293–304.

Gasnier, M. *Le Silence de Saint Joseph*. Paris: Le Laurier, 1996.

Gauthier, R. *Bibliographie sur Saint Joseph et la Sainte Familie*. Montreal: Oratoire Saint-Joseph, 1999.

———. "Der heilige Joseph in der Heilsgeschichte." *Josefstudien*, March 2, 1994: 2–7.

———. *La Paternité de Saint Joseph*. Montreal: Oratoire Saint-Joseph, 1958.

———. "La Proclamation de Saint Joseph comme la Patron de l' Église." *Cahiers de Joséphologie* 43 (1995) 29–50.

———. "Saint Joseph d'aprés les Théologiens de la Fin du XX siècle." In *Cahiers 11 de l'Oratoire Saint Joseph*, 63–81. Montreal: Oratoire Saint-Joseph, 2001.

Gauthier, R., and G. M. Bertrand. *Dictionnaire de Spiritualité*, vol. 8. Paris: Beauchesne, 1975.

Gelin, A. *Les Pauvres que Dieu Aime*. Paris: Cerf, 1967.

George, A., "Pauvre." In *Supplément au Dictionnaire de la Bible VII*, 386–406. Paris: Letouzey et Ané, 1966.

Gerson, J., "Sermo de Nativitate Gloriosae Virginis Mariae." In *Concilio Constantiensi*, Tertia Pars Operum, 2.4:140. Paris: 1606.

Goldstein, H., *Brasilianische Christologie, Jesus der Severino heisst*. Mettingen: Brasilienkunde-Verlag, 1982.

Grelot, P. "Saint Joseph." In *Dictionnaire de Spiritualité*, 8:1289–1301. Paris: Beauchesne, 1974.

Guitton, J. *La Vierge Marie*. Paris: Aubier, 1949.

Gutiérrez, Gustavo. *Power of the Poor in History*. Maryknoll, NY: Orbis, 1979.

———. *A Theology of Liberation: History, Politics, and Salvation*. Rev. ed. Translated and edited by Sister Caridad Inda and John Eagleson. London: SCM, 2001.

Heising, Alkuin. *Gott wird Mensch: Eine Einführung in die Aussageabsicht und Darstellungsweise von Mt 1–2, Lk 1–2; 3,28–38*. Kreuzring-Bücherei 45. Trier: Zimmer, 1967.

Honoré-Lainet, Geneviève. *Il fiat di Giuseppe in cui il Padre si revela*. Milano: 1994

Houdijk, Rinus. "Forms of Cohabitation and Procreation outside Marriage." Translated by John Bowden. *Concilium* (1995) 18–25.

Iglesias, A. L. "La paternidad de San José le relaciona con el orden hipostático." *Estudios Josefinos* 6 (1952) 56–79.

Isolani, Isidore, O.P. *Summa de Donis Sancti Joseph*. Edited by P. Berthier. New ed. Rome, 1807.

Jeremias, Joachim. *Abba: Studien zur neutestamentlichen Theologie und Zeitgeschichte*. Göttingen: Vandenhoeck & Ruprecht, 1966.

———. *Jerusalem in the Time of Jesus*. Translated by F. H. Cave and C. H. Cave. Philadelphia: Fortress, 1969.

———. *Jerusalém no tempo de Jesus: pesquisas de história econômico-social no período neotestamentário*, São Paulo: Paulinas, 1986.

John of Damascus. *De fide orthodoxa*.

John Paul II. Apostolic Exhortation: *Familiaris Consortio.* November 22, 1981.

————. Apostolic Exhortation: *Redemptoris Custos.* August 15, 1989.

————. Letter to Families: *Gratissimam Sane.* February 2, 1994.

Johnson, Marshall D. *The Purpose of the Biblical Genealogies with Special Reference to the Setting of the Genealogies of Jesus.* Society for New Testament Studies Monograph Series 8. 1969. Reprinted, Eugene, OR: Wipf & Stock, 2002.

Jung, C. G. *The Archetypes and the Collective Unconscious.* Princeton: Princeton University Press, 1968.

————. *Die Bedeutung des Vaters für das Schicksal des Einzelnen.* Leipzig: Deuticke, 1909.

————. "Preface." In V. White, *God and the Unconscious.* Cleveland: World, 1961.

————. "A Psychological Approach to the Dogma of the Trinity." In *Collected Works*, vol. 11. Princeton: Princeton University Press, 1970.

————. *Psychology and Religion: West and East.* New York: Pantheon, 1958.

————. *Symbols of Transformation—An Analysis of the Prelude to a Case of Schizophrenia.* Princeton: Princeton University Press, 1967.

Juritsch, M. *Sociologia da Paternidade*, Petrópolis: Vozes, 1970.

Josephus, Flavius. *The Complete Works of Flavius Josephus.* Translated by William Whiston. London: Nelson, 1858.

Kant, Immanuel. *Der Streit der Fakultäten.* Berlin: Reimer, 1917.

————. *The Conflict of Faculties (Der Streit der Fakultäten).* Translated by Mary J. Gregor. 1979. Reprinted, Lincoln: University of Nebraska Press, 1992.

Kelsey, Morton T. *God, Dreams, and Revelation—A Christian Interpretation of Dreams.* Minneapolis: Augsburg, 1973.

Lallement, D.-J. *Mystère de la Paternité de Saint Joseph.* Paris: Téqui, 1986.

Lalonde, M. "La Signification Mystique du Marriage de Joseph et de Marie." *Cahiers de Joséphologie* 19 (1971) 548–57.

Latourelle, René. *Théologie de la Revelation.* Studia: Travaux de Recherche 15. Paris: Desclée de Brouwer, 1963.

————. *Theology of Revelation: Including a Commentary on the Constitution "Dei verbum" of Vatican II.* Staten Island, NY: Alba, 1966.

Laurentin, René. *Les Évangiles de l'Enfance du Christ.* Paris: Desclée de Brouwer, 1982.

————. *The Truth of Christmas beyond the Myths: The Gospels of the Infancy of Christ.* Petersham, MA: St. Bede's, 1986.

Leal, J. "La misión de José en la historia de Jesús." *Manresa*, 41 (1960) 209–16.

Le Guillou, Marie-Joseph. *Il mistero del Padre.* Milano: Jaca, 1979.

Léon-Dufour, Xavier. "L'annonce à Joseph." In *Mélanges bibliques rédigées en l'honneur d'André Robert.* Travaux de l'Institute Catholique de Paris 4. Paris: Bloud & Gay, 1957.

————. *Dictionary of Biblical Theology.* New York: Seabury Press, 1973.

Llamas, R. "Profilo spirituale di San Giuseppe: consideración intorno all'esortacione apostólica Redemptoris Custos." *Rivista di Vita Spirituale* 44 (1990) 138–74.

Llamera, B. "La Relación de San José con el Orden Hipostático." *Estudios Josefinos* 1 (1947) 34–64.

————. "Pertenece San José al Orden Hipostático?" *Ciencia Tomista* 71 (1946) 251–81.

————. *Teología de San José*. Madrid: BAC, 1953.

Margoliouth, Moses. *A Pilgrimage to the Land of My Fathers*. 2 vols. London: Bentley, 1850.

Maria, José Jesús de, OCD. "Bibliografía fundamental josefina." *Estudios Josefinos* 20 (1966) 14–23, 28–31, 40–50, 54–56.

Martelet, Bernard. *Joseph de Nazareth: L'Homme de Confiance*. Paris: Saint-Paul, 1974.

————. *Joseph, Fils de David: Qui êtes-vous?* Nouan-le-Fuselier: Lion de Juda, 1987.

McGinnis, T. "The Holiness of St. Joseph and the Order of the Hypostatic Union." In *The Marian Forum, The Praise of St Joseph*, 1:14–23. New York: Scapular, 1961.

McManaman, D., "St. Joseph Care and the Ordinary: A Brief Look at the Life Issues in View of St. Joseph's Fatherhood." *Cahiers de Joséphologie* 38 (1990) 115–26.

Ménard, G. M. *Saint Joseph et l'Esprit Saint*. Montreal, 1983.

Mendel, Gérard. *La Révolte contre le Père: Une Introduction à la Socio-Pschanalyse*. Paris: Payot, 1971.

Mersters, C. "Origen dos Quatro Evangelhos: Do Evangelho aos Quatro Evangelhos." In *Deus, onde estás?* 125–28. Petrópolis: Vozes, 2003.

Michel, A. "Appartenance de S. Joseph à l'ordre de l'union hypostatique." *L'ami du clergé* 66 (1956) 177–83.

Mitscherlich, Alexander. *Auf dem Weg zur vaterlossen Gesellschaft: Ideen zur Sozialpsychologie*. Sammlung Piper: Probleme und Ergebnisse der modernen Wissenschaft. Munich: Piper, 1963.

Moltmann, Jürgen. *The Way of Jesus Christ: Christology in Messianic Dimensions*. Translated by Margaret Kohl. San Francisco: HarperSanFrancisco, 1990.

————. "The Motherly Father: Is Trinitarian Patripassianism Replacing Theological Patriarchalism?" *Concilium* 143 (1981) 51–56.

Monferrer Sala, Juana Pedro. "Evangelho Àrabe de la Infancia." In *Textos Apócrifos àrabes cristianos*. Madrid: Trotta, 2003.

Monforte, J. *José de Nazaret et el Tercer Milenio Cristiano*. Madrid: Eunsa, 2001.

Morales, Petrus. *In caput primum Matthaei, de Christo Domino, Sanctissima Virgine Deipara Maria, Veroque eius Dulcissimo & Virginali Sponso Iosepho, Libri Quinque*. Lugduni: Cardon, 1614.

Moran, Gabriel. *Theology of Revelation*. Studies in Religious Education. New York: Herder & Herder, 1969.

Moreira de Azevedo, E. B., and L. M. Moreira de Azevedo. *Matrimônio: Para que Serve este Sacramento?* Petrópolis: Vozes, 1997.

O'Carroll, Michael. *Joseph, Son of David*. Dublin: Gill, 1963.

Oehl, W. *"Das fliessende Licht der Gottheit."* In *Auswahl*. Deutsche Mystiker 2 Kempten: Kösel, 1911.

Olier, Jean-Jacques. *Oeuvres Completes: Réunies pour la Premiere Fois en Collection*. Paris: Migne, 1856.

Origen. *Contra Celsum*.

Palmier, S. "Pertenencia de San José al Orden de la Unión Hipostática." *Estudios Josefinos* 12 (1958) 36–62.

Peralta, Antonio. *Dissertationes Scholasticae de Sancto Joseph*. Mexico, 1727.

Pessoa, Fernando. *The Keeper of Sheep*. Translated by Edwin Honig and Susan M Brown. Riverdale-on-Hudson, NY: Sheep Meadow, 1985.

Perrin, J. *Une Juste Nommé Joseph*. Paris: Mediaspaul, 1985.

Perrot, C. *Les Récites de l'Enfance de Jésus*. Paris: Cerf, 1976.

Perrota, Louise Bourassa. *Saint Joseph: His Life and His Role in the Church*. Huntington, IN: Our Sunday Visitor, 2000.

Piccirelli, G. M. "Della preminenza assoluta di San Giuseppe nell'ordine extrínseco dell'unione hipostatica." *Bolletino della Lega Sacerdotale* (1890–91).

———. *San Giuseppe nell'Ordine Presente della Divina Providenza: Se ed in che Senso puo dirsi Appartenere San Giuseppe all'Ordine dell'Unione Hipostatica—Disquisizione Teologica*. Castellamare di Stabia: Tipografia San Martino, 1897.

Pixley, Jorge, and Clovodis Boff. *Opção Pelos Pobres*. Petrópolis: Vozes, 1987.

———. *The Bible, the Church, and the Poor*. Translated by Paul Burns. Maryknoll, NY: Orbis, 1989.

Pohier, J.-M. *Au Nom du Père: Recherches Théologiques et Psychanalytiques*. Cogatatio Fidei 66. Paris: Cerf, 1972.

Poutet, Yves. "Saint Joseph dans la Spiritualité de l'Assemblée des Amis (AA) au XVII Siècle." In *La Figure de Joseph à l'Orée du Troisième Millénaire*, 101–19. Cahiers de l'Oratoire Saint Joseph 6. Montreal: Centre de Recherce et de Documentation, Oratoire Saint-Joseph, 1999.

Pujiula, J. "Aptitud de San José para el Orden Hipostático." *Revista San José de la Montaña, Barcelona* 47 (1951) 55–56; 100–101.

Ramos, Lincoln. *Biblia Apocrifa: A Paixao de Jesus nos Escritos Secretos*. Petrópolis: Vozes, 1990.

Rasco, E. "El Anuncio a José (Mt 1, 18-25)." *Cahiers de Joséphologie* 19 (1960) 81–103.

Resch, Andreas. *Der Traum im Heilsplan Gottes: Deutung und Bedetung des Traumes im Alten Testament*. Freiburg: Herder, 1964.

Ricouer, Paul. "La Paternité: Du Fantasme au Symbole." In *L'analyse du Langage Théologique: Le Nom de Dieu. Acts du Colloque Organisé par le Centre International d'Études Humanistes et par l'Institut d'Études Philosophiques de Rome. Rome, 5–11 Janvier 1969. Aux soins de Enrico Castelli*, 221–46. Paris: Aubier, 1969.

Riedl, Johannes. *Die Vorgeschichte Jesu: Die Heilbotschaft von Mt 1-2 und Lk 1-2*. Biblisches Forum 3. Stuttgart: Katholisches Bibelwerk, 1968.

Risé, C. "Alla Ricerca del Padre." *L'Officina*, 2 (2005) 46-50.

———. *Il padre: l'Assente Innaccettabile*. Rome: San Paolo, 2003.

———. "L'Occidente senza Padre." *Da Area* 73 (2003).

Robert, P. "Joseph de Bethléem et la Spiritualité des Pauvres de Yahvé." In *La Figure de Joseph à l'Orée du Troisième Millénaire*, 69–100. Cahiers de l'Oratoire Saint Joseph 6. Montreal: Centre de Recherce et de Documentation, Oratoire Saint-Joseph, 1999.

Rochais, G. "La figure de Joseph dans les Récites de l'Enfance selon Saint Matthieu." In *La Figure de Joseph à l'Orée du Troisième Millénaire*, 21–37. Cahiers de l'Oratoire Saint Joseph 6. Montreal: Centre de Recherce et de Documentation, Oratoire Saint-Joseph, 1999.

Roman de La Immaculada, OCA. "Pertenencia de San José al orden de la unión hipostática." *Estudios Josefinos* 10 (1956) 147–56.

Rondet, H. "Saint Joseph, histoire et théologie." *Nouvelle Revue Théologique* (1953).

———. *Saint Joseph: Textes Anciennes avec une Introduction*. Paris: Lethillieux, 1953.

Rosanas, J. *Teologia de San José*. Buenos Aires, 1949.

Sala, J. P. M. "Historia de José, el carpinteiro." In *Apócrifos àrabes cristianos*. Madrid: Trotta, 2003.

Samson, H. "San Giuseppe e l'ordine dell'unione ipostatica." *Movimento Giuseppino* 10 (abr. 1966) 8-18.

Sanabria, J. R. "Le mysterieux silence de Saint Joseph." In *Cahiers 11 de l'Oratoire Saint Joseph*, 9–22. Montreal: Oratoire Saint-Joseph, 2001.

Sanford, J. A. *Dreams: God's Forgotten Language*. New York: HarperSanFrancisco, 1988.

Santos Otero, A. *Los Evangelios Apócrifos*. Madrid: BAC, 1948.

Sauvé, C. *Le Mystère de Joseph*. Nice: Agneau, 1978.

Schillebeeckx, Edward. *Marriage: Human Reality and Saving Mystery*. Translated by N. D. Smith. New York: Sheed & Ward, 1965.

———. *O matrimônio: realidade terrestre e mistério de salvação*. Petrópolis: Vozes, 1980.

Schnackenburg, Rudolf. "A Ressureição de Jesus Cristo como ponto histórico da fé em Cristo." In *Mysterium Salutis* III/2: 8–15. Petrópolis: Vozes, 1973.

Schumaker, Adauto. "A Trindade mediadora—Primícias da redenção." Unpublished manuscript. March 19, 1987.

Schreder, F. S. "S. Joseph et l'Union Hypostatique." (In Polish) *Ruch Biblijny i Liturgiczny* 27 (1974) 215–20.

Segundo, Juan Luis. *A História Perdida e Recuperada de Jesus de Nazaré*. São Paulo: Paulus, 1997.

Seitz, Joseph. *Die Verehrung des hl. Joseph in ihrer geschichtlichen Entwicklung bis zum Konzil von Trient dargestellt*. Freiburg: Herder, 1908.

Shoemaker, Stephen J. *Ancient Traditions of the Virgin Mary's Dormition and Assumption*. Oxford: Oxford University Press, 2002.

Sicari, A. "Joseph Justus (Mt 1, 19): La Storia dell'interpretazione e le Nuove Prospettive." *Cahiers de Joséphologie* 19 (1960) 53–61.

Siuta, D. D. "Saint Joseph et les Crises de la Vie." In *La Figure de Joseph à l'Orée du Troisième Millénaire*, 51–68. Cahiers de l'Oratoire Saint Joseph 6. Montreal: Centre de Recherce et de Documentation, Oratoire Saint-Joseph, 1999.

Sobrino, Jon. *Christology at the Crossroads: A Latin American Approach*. Translated by John Drury. Maryknoll, NY: Orbis, 1978.

Solá i Carrio, F. P. "Pertenencia de San José al Orden Hipostático." *Estudios Josefinos* 16 (1962) 129–46.

Spicq, Ceslas. "Joseph, son mari, étant juste (Mt 1, 19)." *Revue Biblique* 71 (1964) 206–14.

Squillaci, D. "Matrimonio di S. Giuseppe (Mt 1, 19)." *Palestra Del Clero* 42 (1963) 659–66.

Stöhr, Johannes. "Zur Theologie und Verehrung des heiligen Joseph in Deutschland seit der Säkularisation. " *Josefstudien*, March 2, 1994: 8–14.

Stramare, Tarcisio. *Figlio di Giuseppe da Nazaret: Problemi dell'Infanzia di Gesú.* Rovigo: Instituto Padano di Arti Grafiche, 1972.

———. "Giuseppe." In *Nuovo Dizionario di Mariología,* edited by Stefano De Fiores and Salvatore Meo, 633–55. Milan: Paoline, 1985.

———. "I Sogni di S. Giuseppe." *Cahiers de Joséphologie* 19 (1971) 104–22.

———. *San Giuseppe nella S. Scrittura, nella Teologia e nel Culto.* Rome: Piemmi, 1983.

———. *Vangelo dei Misteri della Vita Nascota di Gesú.* Bibbia e Oriente Supplementa 7. Bornato in Franciacorta: Sardini, 1998.

Suárez, F. "Comentarium in Tertiam (of Saint Thomas Aquinas' Summa Theologica), q. 29, a. 2, disp. 8, sectio I, n. 10." In *Opera Omnia,* vol. 19. Paris: Vivès, 1860.

Suenens, Léon-Joseph. "Saint Joseph et le Renouveau Familial." *L'église en marche,* March 11, 1962.

Tardan-Masquelier, Ysé. *Jung: La Sacralité de l'Expérience Intérieure.* Reperes dans un Nouvel. Paris: Droguet et Ardant, 1992.

Teresa of Avila. *The Life of Saint Theresa of Avila by Herself.* Translated with an introduction by J. M. Cohen. Penguin Classics. New York: Penguin, 1957.

Theissen, Gerd, and Annette Merz. *The Historical Jesus: A Comprehensive Guide.* Minneapolis: Fortress, 1998.

———. *O Jesus Histórico: Um Manual.* São Paulo: Loyola, 2002.

Thomas Aquinas. *Summa Theologica III.*

Trilling, Wolfgang. *Jesús y los Problemas de su Historicidad.* Barcelona: Herder, 1970.

Vidal, M. *Moral das Atitudes.* 4 vols. São Paulo: Paulinas, 1991–94.

———. *Moral do Matrimônio.* Petrópolis: Vozes, 1982.

Vischer, Wilhelm. "Comment Arriva la Naissance de Jésus-Christ? Méditation sur le Rôle de Joseph selon Mt 1, 25." *Études théologiques et religieuses* 37 (1962) 365–70.

Walker, Alexander, translator. *Apocryphal Gospels, Acts and Revelations.* Edinburgh: T. & T. Clark, 1870.

Winnicott, D. W. *The Child, the Family and the Outside World.* London: Penguin, 1964.

———. *The Family and Individual Development.* New York: Routledge, 2006.

———. *Talking to Parents.* Reading, MA: Addison-Wesley, 1993.

WEB SITES

www.earlychristianwritings.com

www.jozefologia.pl/bibliografia.htm

www.hebrew4christians.com

www.microbookstudio.com

www.newadvent.org

www.redemptoriscustos.org/bibliof_es.html

www.vatican.va

Scripture Index

OLD TESTAMENT

www.ingramcontent.com/pod-product-compliance
Lightning Source LLC
Chambersburg PA
CBHW030307100426
42812CB00002B/603